## Acknowledgements

This book is dedicated to my

It was written with the love
Adrian, and our daughters Melinda, Emily and Alyrene.

I would like to thank my friends Jill and Dave who feature
in the book and my brother, Nigel. They have helped me
delve back to memories of a very different time.

Special thanks are due to Shawn White for the cover
design and Caroline White for her insightful editing and
proof reading.

My thanks are also due to all my writer friends especially
Oxford Writers Group who have been a continual source of
advice and encouragement and to Writers at Blackwell's.

## About the Author

Heather Rosser spent twelve years working in Africa as a teacher, researcher and journalist. She met her husband, Adrian, in Ghana and they travelled to Timbuktu together. After they married they returned to West Africa. Heather's work as a teacher and researcher in Nigeria in the 1970s brought her into close contact with a variety of cultures and customs, many of which are no longer practised. In the 1980s Heather and Adrian lived in Botswana with their three young daughters where they continued to forge life-long friendships.

On their return to Britain they bought a smallholding in Lincolnshire where Heather ran a language school specialising in English courses for Development Workers preparing for overseas postings.

Since moving to Oxford, Heather has written Social Studies text books for African Primary Schools.

She has a particular interest in documenting family memoir. Her historical novel, *In the Line of Duty*, was published in 2014 and is based on her grandfather's experience as a seaplane pilot in the First World War.

Heather has drawn on her diaries, letters and photographs in the writing of *Growing up in the Mandara Mountains*.

website
**www.heatherrosser.com**

# Contents

# Map 1 Nigeria 1967-1976

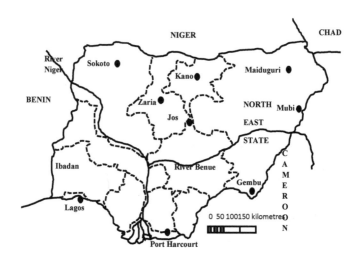

# Map 2 Places visited in North East State 1972-1976

# Foreword

In the 1970s, Mubi was a remote border town on the foothills of the Mandara Mountains where small hill tribes lived in harmony with their neighbours from the plains. Muslims, Christians and Animists were free to practise their religions and foreigners, especially from neighbouring Cameroon, were welcomed.

When I arrived in Nigeria with my husband, Adrian, we could feel the optimism as people looked forward to an era of peace after the bitter Civil War. We were posted to Mubi Teacher Training College but I had to give up my job after the birth of our daughter, Melinda. I decided to document pregnancy and childbirth customs among the Gude who were the main tribe of that area of the Mandara.

Travelling with my baby on my back I spoke to men and women from different religions and beliefs. As well as meeting local government officers and medical staff, I was privileged to be invited into the homes of some of our students who introduced me to their families and community leaders including tribal chiefs and traditional doctors as well Christian and Muslim religious leaders.

The book begins with Melinda's dramatic introduction to Adrian when we arrived in Kano just five weeks after she was born in England. Although we lived in Mubi for four years, this memoir concentrates on the eighteen months from December 1974 – July 1976.

It has not been possible to mention all our friends and colleagues during our time in the North East of Nigeria. In this memoir, I have mainly mentioned those who shared my interest in finding out about the local customs. Neither have I mentioned by name everyone I interviewed, although there is a table of respondents in the appendix. Letters, diary extracts and articles are also included.

The easy relationship between Nigerians and ex-pats, Muslims and Christians was a feature of our life at that time. Many of the market traders worshipped traditional gods and natural features of the landscape. The term used then, both by themselves and others, was Pagan so that is the term I have used throughout this book.

Since I started writing the memoir the Mandara Mountains is no longer a peaceful place to live. Mubi and the villages I used to visit have endured attacks and bombing from Boko Haram and other insurgents. By describing how things used to be I hope that, in a small way, I have shown that it is possible for people of differing customs and religions to believe in a better future.

# Glossary

| | |
|---|---|
| **Alhaji** | Hausa - Muslim who has completed the pilgrimage to Mecca |
| **baturi** | Hausa - white man |
| **ba kome** | Hausa - doesn't matter, no worries |
| **calabash** | containers and drums made from gourds produced by the calabash plant |
| **durbar** | Islamic festival usually involving a parade of horsemen to celebrate the end of a period of religious fasting. |
| | may also refer to a charge of horsemen welcoming important guests |
| **Emir** | Islamic ruler |
| **finial** | ornament at apex of a roof |
| **Haba** | Hausa - exclamation of surprise or sympathy |
| **Haj** | annual Islamic pilgrimage to Mecca |
| **Hausa** | largest ethnic group in Northern Nigeria and neighbouring countries |
| | language spoken by Hausa people and the lingua franca of Northern Nigeria |
| **Igbo** | largest ethnic group of South East Nigeria |
| | language spoken by Igbo people |
| **Imam** | Muslim priest |
| **Lamido** | traditional Islamic ruler, word originates in Fulfulde language in West Africa |
| **laterite** | hard red soil used to make bricks and roads. |
| **kana lafiya?** | Hausa - How are you? |
| **lafyia lau** | Hausa - I am well |
| **mallam** | learned man or scribe |
| **nagode** | Hausa – thank you |
| **Ramadan** | the ninth month of the Muslim year, during which strict fasting is observed from dawn to sunset |
| **riga** | gown worn by men |

| | |
|---|---|
| **Sallah Eid ul Fitr** | celebration and prayers at the end of Ramadan |
| **Sannu** | Hausa greeting |
| **Taureg** | traditionally nomadic pastoralists living in the Sahara and sub-Saharan region |
| **TTC** | Teacher Training College |
| **Yoruba** | largest ethnic group in Western and parts of Central Nigeria |
| | language spoken by Yoruba people |

# Sannu de zuwa – Welcome

Clasping Melinda in my arms I stood unsteadily on the top step of the Boeing 707. It was December 1974 and we had left the damp darkness of England six hours earlier. My eyes were heavy with lack of sleep and I blinked uncomprehendingly at the robed figures squatting by small fires at the airport perimeter. I was unaware that it was Ramadan and the shadowy figures were pilgrims awaiting their plane to Mecca. According to custom they were eating before the dawn broke, heralding another day of fasting.

The air stewardess began to fidget behind me as I stood rooted to the spot. At only five-and-a-half weeks, Melinda was by far the youngest on board but we had been overlooked. All the other passengers for Kano had disembarked while I sat patiently waiting for someone to help me with the paraphernalia that inevitably travels with a baby.

'But I thought you were going on to Lagos!' the stewardess said as she bundled us out of our seat.

I glanced at Melinda, wrapped in her beautifully crocheted shawl and looking wide-eyed as she absorbed the scents and sounds of Africa.

Suddenly I heard a shout and there was Adrian leaping up the steps and hugging us as he met his daughter for the first time.

'How the devil did he get here?' The captain had joined the stewardess to find out what the commotion was about.

Words were exchanged about the airline's responsibility to their passengers but nothing more was said about the security breach that had enabled Adrian to rush through several barriers and onto the runway.

Immigration and customs were cleared with surprisingly little fuss, partly because Adrian's pride in his new baby was infectious but probably also because the officials were anxious to go home for their breakfast.

Dawn was breaking as we drove out of the airport past goats nibbling at scrubby vegetation. As we entered the city we passed the groundnut processing factory. It felt as if we had stuck our noses in a jar of peanut butter and the cloying scent remained throughout our short stay at Kano's Central Hotel.

The following day we set off for Mubi, travelling south then heading east across the Bauchi plain towards the Mandara Mountains.

# Chapter 1    A Bush Posting

My first sight of Nigeria was in September 1972 when we touched down in Kano before continuing to the semi-desert capital of the North East State.

Our luggage had been lost somewhere between London and Maiduguri so Adrian and I were staying at Lake Chad Hotel waiting for it to arrive. Wishing I had something appropriate to change into, we joined a group of ex-pats by the pool who wanted to know where we were heading.

'I believe yours is a bush posting,' said the wife of the Permanent Secretary for Education when we said we were going to Mubi.

That wasn't how her husband had described Mubi when he and two Nigerian officials on the interview panel had offered us teaching appointments in the English and Science departments at the Teacher Training College. Maybe our year's VSO teaching in Ghana had recommended us for what many people, including Nigerians, thought of as a remote place with few facilities.

'You'll need to stock up on essentials while you're here,' she continued.

Her friend nodded in agreement. 'There's no cold store in Mubi, you had better buy a large cool box for dairy products. It will be useful for the journey anyway - you must make sure you take plenty of water. I assume you're planning on buying a car here?'

'We're hoping to,' said Adrian.

'There's a Renault dealer that had a new consignment recently. Their vehicles are good on bush roads.'

Five days later we picked up our car and drove south-east across the Maiduguri Plain to Bama where the tarmac road ended. As we headed south the laterite road began to climb towards the rocky outcrops of the Mandara Mountains. By the time we reached Gwoza we felt like a break but did not stop. We had heard tales of hostility towards strangers and so we continued along the dusty

11

road until we came to a couple of roadside stalls.

There was a strong smell of cooking as we got out of the car. We smiled at an elderly woman who was stirring meat in a pot over a small fire but shook our heads when she offered some for sale. Next to her was a woman wearing a brightly patterned wrapper and headscarf. She spoke rapidly and pointed to the fruit carefully laid out in front of her. I picked up two oranges and bananas then, using sign language, we agreed on a price and I counted out the kobo she asked for.

The elderly woman asked a question and pointed south.

'Mubi,' I said, hoping that I had correctly guessed she was asking where we were going.

She let out an exclamation and shook her head but the younger women smiled and gave what appeared to be advice for the journey as she waved us on our way.

Beginning to wonder what we had signed up for, I turned my attention to the car.

'How is she to drive?' I asked as Adrian speeded up on a straight piece of road.

'The French know how to make cars for these roads. You'll love her. And she'll go much faster than the Dyane 4.'

We both chuckled at the memory of the little car we had reluctantly sold just before leaving for Nigeria.

The vegetation became lusher and the rock formations more spectacular as we travelled south.

'Look!' I said suddenly.

Running towards us were four men, each holding a corner of a grass roof. A tall man in a white caftan and red pill box style hat strode behind them and, running slightly behind him, was a young boy carrying a large suitcase on his head.

'That's an interesting way to move house!' said Adrian as we inched our way past and I felt a tingle of excitement about the possibility of new and interesting experiences in this remote part of Nigeria.

\*\*\*

It was late afternoon by the time we arrived in Mubi. Following the instructions we had been given at the Ministry of Education, we drove slowly through the town. Taking care to avoid goats, people and motor cycles, we passed the mosque and the church then crossed a single track bridge over a wide river bed with just a trickle of water meandering through.

We followed the road uphill past the Ministry of Works, government offices and the government residential area then turned in at the entrance to the College. On one side of the driveway was a football pitch and on the other were three bungalows half hidden behind tall trees and bushes.

At the end of the drive was a rectangle of earth delineated by white painted stones and in the centre was a flag pole with the green and white Nigerian flag scarcely moving in the still air.

Adrian parked outside a single storey building and we looked through the open door. A young Nigerian in slacks and a short sleeved shirt was sitting at one of the tables surrounded by books. He smiled in welcome when we explained we were new teachers and said that he was also new and was preparing some lessons for the beginning of term.

'Mr Wade is in the office.' He indicated a door at the end of the staff room.

We knocked and an English voice called us to come in. A man in his early thirties wearing a brightly coloured shirt took off his glasses and studied us for a moment then put out his hand.

'Jim Wade, Deputy Principal,' he said as he shook hands.

'Adrian and Heather Rosser,' we replied formally.

'Did you drive?'

'Yes, our car's outside.'

'Let's go then.' He picked up some keys and handed

13

them to us. 'I asked the District Office to send these over in case you arrived after they closed. Now, if you give me a lift, I'll take you to your accommodation. We're waiting for more staff houses to be built but for the moment you'll be living in the old District Commissioner's house.'

Several of the bungalows we drove past had beds of scarlet calla lilies which gave a vivid splash of colour to the parched gardens.

'You can pull in here,' said Jim as we came to a low colonial style building with white washed walls and green paintwork round the windows and doors. Shrubs and dried grass indicated that the garden had not been tended for a while but several tall mahogany trees gave welcome shade.

As we got out of the car I caught sight of movement in one of the trees. Then my eye was drawn to a woman sitting on the ground surrounded by nuts the size of tennis balls. Her head was shaved and, apart from a girdle of leaves around her waist and a bead necklace, she was naked.

Jim was unperturbed.

'They're collecting mahogany nuts for the oil,' he told us and proceeded to talk to the woman in a language I did not recognise. Despite my limited time in the country, I knew it wasn't Hausa, the lingua franca of Northern Nigeria.

There was a rustling of leaves followed by a hail of nuts then the figure in the tree began to climb down. She didn't appear bothered by our presence and greeted us with a smile which showed her teeth stained red from eating cola nuts.

'These ladies are from the Gude tribe,' said Jim. 'It's their custom to harvest mahogany nuts at this time of year.'

I suddenly thought that my father would soon be putting up his ladder to pick apples from the tree in their garden in Surrey.

The women packed the nuts into their calabashes, hoisted them on their heads and disappeared into a tangle

14

of tall grasses and bushes at what appeared to be the boundary of our garden.

'Welcome to the people of the Mandara,' said Jim with a wry smile. 'Life can be interesting here. I believe you worked in Ghana. Did you travel much while you were there?'

'We went to Timbuktu', we said in unison.

He nodded. 'Then I guess you know how to look after yourselves. I think you'll enjoy teaching here because you'll get the chance to go to the villages when our students are on teaching practice.'

'That was one of the things that attracted us,' I said.

'Good. Now, the important things...' He pointed to a building with tables and chairs outside. 'That's the Club next door and the Rest House is opposite so you'll be the first to know who's visiting town. I suggest you eat there this evening'

He handed us the key. 'I'll leave you to it then.'

# Chapter 2    Hazel gets her wish

Jim had been right about the opportunities to visit the surrounding villages when our students were on teaching practice and I wrote enthusiastic letters home describing life in the Mandara Mountains. When I was a child my parents, Hazel and Ray, had looked forward to my godmother's letters from Nigeria and now I was following in her footsteps. They wanted to know all about our life in Mubi when we were on leave the following year so, on the spur of the moment, we invited them to spend Christmas with us.

Mum and Dad flew to Kano in December 1973 and for the next four weeks were able to forget the miseries of power cuts, the coal miners' strike and Britain's 'three day week' which lasted most of the winter.

They exclaimed in delight when we drove slowly out of the airport past a man wearing a dark blue caftan and leading two camels.

Later we visited the dye pits where men squatted over circular brick pits plunging fabrics into water infused with indigo. Further on, we watched a Taureg bargaining with one of the dyers over a piece of cloth.

'Did you notice, the man's hands were blue,' said Dad as we walked away.

My parents were interested in everything and Dad meticulously recorded what he had seen each day in his diary.

From Kano we drove to Jos where we stayed for a couple of days before continuing to Mubi. The laterite roads threw up clouds of red dust so we kept our windows closed and were all sweating throughout the long journey.

As the day wore on, we were beginning to feel fidgety.

'Is everyone okay?' asked Adrian.

I glanced at Mum who was tapping her foot on the floor.

'I think we need to stretch our legs,' I said.

Soon afterwards Adrian slowed down as we approached a small town. We pulled up outside a bar advertising Star beer. I could feel sweat running down my legs and my hands were sticky.

'Do you think they have a toilet?' Mum asked.

Adrian spoke to the barman who had come to greet us and admire our car.

'He says there is a toilet round the back.' Adrian looked doubtful then proceeded to answer questions from the little crowd who were gathering around the car.

Mum and I went to investigate but returned quickly, having been put off by flies buzzing round a hole in the ground behind flimsy corrugated iron sheeting.

'Would you like some warm Coke?' Dad asked and held up his latest purchase.

Mum hesitated.

'I think she'd prefer cold water,' I said and poured some water from the Coleman water cooler that we took with us on every car journey.

Feeling refreshed, we continued on our way. As we came closer to Mubi I pointed out some of the villages where our students did their teaching practice. Half an hour later the road surface turned to tarmac.

'Welcome to Mubi!' I said as we drove through the town to the College.

I wound down my window and pointed. 'This is the main entrance; the new houses are a bit further on.'

Mum craned her neck and broke into a broad smile as we drove slowly into the area of new staff houses, each surrounded by an attempt at a garden.

The sun had set a few minutes earlier but we could just make out our bed of marigolds dancing as if in welcome as we came to a halt.

Suddenly the porch was flooded with light and Ahmadu, our steward, came out to greet my parents.

\*\*\*

Mum and Dad slept well and were eager to see their surroundings.

'We'll start with the college,' I said. 'We need to pop into the staff room to collect our post.'

The classrooms were locked but Adrian had a key for the science laboratory and Dad was particularly interested as Adrian showed us round.

Mum wanted to know where the students slept and we pointed out the new dormitory block then took them to an area of thatched huts.

'This is where all the students slept originally,' I said, 'but now we have more students these huts are reserved for the fifth formers.'

'They have nice views,' said Mum pointing across the playing field to the mountains in the distance.

'We'll take the short cut back.' Adrian led the way through some trees to our little estate of houses.

We passed two bungalows, older and bigger than ours and surrounded by trees and shrubs. 'That's where Helen and Keith our Canadian friends live,' I said. 'They've gone to Maiduguri for supplies, you'll see them tomorrow.'

A couple of hens scratched the earth in front of us and a young boy was kicking a football. He stopped and smiled shyly when I greeted him.

'That's one of Mr Oyiypo's children. He's a senior teacher and his wife works at one of the local primary schools.'

A couple of minutes later we were sitting comfortably in the shade at the back of our house with glasses of iced tea. I pointed to the track at the bottom of the garden and told my parents that it was the main route by foot and occasionally donkey from the hill villages to Mubi. On market days it was particularly busy with people from the Gude and Fali tribes going to sell their wares. As we drank our tea a woman stopped and lifted down the basket she was carrying on her head then brought out a brightly coloured cloth which she wrapped around her body, covering her leaf apron.

18

Mum and Dad were intrigued when I said that on their return from market the women stopped to pick handfuls of bright green leaves, then they packed away their wrapper, discarded their old leaves and fastened the fresh leaves around their waist. They were surprised when I told them that one of our colleagues from another part of Nigeria thought the women were acting immorally.

'But that's their tradition,' said Dad.

'There's lots of that here.' I stood up. 'Are you ready to go to the market?'

*** 

We drove into town and turned onto a dirt road. Adrian parked outside a small general store and I saw the surprise on Mum's face when I said we were now in the main shopping area.

'We get tinned food and other stuff from here and the bank's next door.' I pointed to the Barclays Bank sign on a small building with a tin roof.

Standing outside was a policeman holding an old Ross rifle.

'Do they expect problems with bank robbers?' asked Dad.

'I don't think so,' said Adrian. 'It's quite secure and is guarded day and night.'

We followed a woman carrying a basket on her head laden with leafy vegetables. Dad took an intake of breath as we entered the market and were bombarded by a cacophony of voices in different languages as well as lowing, bleating and squawking from various livestock for sale.

We wandered round, pausing to look at exotic fruit and vegetables, flamboyant displays of java print cloth, locally made clay cooking pots and brightly coloured enamel dishes from China. My parents were particularly fascinated by a stall selling local medicine. Later, Dad listed in his diary some of the goods for sale which included porcupine quills, a crocodile snout, a dried crow, seed pods and several types of bark.

It was getting hot and I was about to suggest it was time to leave when we noticed three men sitting cross-legged in a secluded corner of the market. On the ground in front of them were several items made of bronze. We stooped down to get a closer look and saw a hand bell, some figurines and several bangles.

'Fascinating!' said Dad as one of the traders handed him the largest bangle. He examined the pattern carved around the side. 'It's intricate work,' he said and handed it to Mum.

'It's rather heavy, we have to be careful about our weight on the return flight.' Mum looked doubtfully at the object and passed it to me.

Despite the heat, the bangle felt cool in my cupped hands as I wondered about the special occasion it had been worn for and how it became to be offered for sale here.

'Do you like it?' asked Adrian.

I slipped it onto my wrist. 'Yes, I don't know if I'd wear it but I like the craftsmanship.'

Adrian started to bargain and fifteen minutes later the bronze bangle was mine.

I smiled as we made our way towards the car. 'I think we're ready for lunch and an afternoon siesta,' I said.

***

In the evening we drove the short distance to the Club, pointing out the old District Commissioner's house that had been our home when we first arrived. We introduced Mum and Dad to our ex-pat and Nigerian friends including Alhaji Ahmadu, the hospital secretary, and Joel the manager of Barclays bank.

Dad was particularly interested in Jimmy, a Nigerian army officer, and wrote in his diary: *'A very pleasant young officer with a somewhat direct approach to problems.'* Two years later we heard that Jimmy was in hiding after an abortive coup in which General Murtala Muhammed, the Head of State, was assassinated.

We never did find out what happened to Jimmy but the Club was an important source of news and gossip where people of different nationalities, tribes and religion met on mutual ground. It was at the Club that we learned about the part Mubi had played in Nigeria's civil war when, despite its majority Muslim population, it gave protection to Christian Igbos fleeing the killings further north.

\*\*\*

We exchanged presents on Christmas morning and friends called round to wish us a Happy Christmas. After their busy few days, Mum and Dad enjoyed relaxing and celebrating our time together with a traditional Christmas Day meal. On Boxing Day they met more of our colleagues at a party given by the British principal of the college and his wife.

That year the Muslim festival of Eid ul-Fitr, or Salah as it was called, followed soon after Christmas. It was observed at the end of Ramadan when the new moon was sighted by the Sultan of Sokoto after a month of fasting.

Mum and Dad showed no hesitation when we suggested getting up early to join the non-Muslims who gathered by some rocks overlooking the river to watch the celebrations. On the other side of the river was the town and football field where a couple of thousand male worshippers were assembling. Boys in their best clothes walked proudly beside their fathers who wore brightly embroidered hats and loose flowing caftans, or rigas as they were also called, in many different colours. From time to time a horseman would wend his way across the river bed, his horse garlanded with woollen tassels of scarlet, orange and emerald green. The riders were often turbaned and sat on richly stitched blankets, many bearing swords or spears. A steady stream of men, women and children walked over the bridge into town and past a lone policeman posted to keep the peace.

Once the call to prayer was heard the worshippers knelt down and touched the ground with their foreheads. This was repeated several times. We watched the proceedings respectfully but, each time the devout congregation bowed down there was derisive laughter from a group of Pagans sitting near us. This made us feel uncomfortable and we decided it was time to see what was happening in town.

When the worship finished the assembly dispersed and we joined the crowd on its way to the town square. The Emir, clad in white and wearing a white turban, was seated on a horse at the front of the procession. Beside him a bodyguard dressed in red held a brightly coloured parasol to protect him from the sun. Behind were several dozen horsemen, some with swords held aloft. Drummers, including both elders and schoolboys, brought up the rear. There was an ebb and flow of enthusiastic onlookers but we decided to find a shady place to watch the proceedings so we hurried on to the town square. This was bounded on two sides by the Emir's palace and on another by the mosque; both buildings were mud-walled and the surface compacted sand.

We sat on a couple of stone steps. 'Sannuku', we said to the men squatting next to us. 'Yauwa sannu,' they replied courteously. There were a couple of other white faces in the crowd but my father began to attract particular interest.

He later recorded in his diary: *'The proceedings started by the appearance of a jester cum MC who was dressed in an embroidered grey caftan and long green hat. He sang and danced around, shaking a single maraca type instrument. At one point the jester removed his grey caftan to reveal underneath a bright orange one, which after more dancing he stripped off to reveal a maroon one. He continued to dance around singing and jesting, some of the time very obviously at our expense.'*

Reading my father's diary many years later I was shocked by the word jester. Living in Nigeria as we did, we knew that the man was a praise singer. However, despite our rudimentary Hausa, we also knew that he was only pretending to sing praises to the elderly white man sitting incongruously among the elders of the local tribes. From the sympathetic looks some of them gave we realised that they also felt uncomfortable when the praise singer knelt in front of Dad in mock adulation, but then - they knew what he was saying.

We were relieved when the sound of a horn heralded the Emir's arrival. By this time the square was a mass of people and the entrance was blocked. A wooden step was placed by the Emir's horse. He dismounted and was accompanied to his seat very close to where we were sitting.

Chiefs from the surrounding villages lined up for a durbar in the Emir's honour. Initially the horses were three abreast, each kicking up the dust and thundering across the square with eyes flashing and nostrils flared as they came to a halt in front of the Emir. However, by the finale they were about twelve abreast and, as the hooves pounded and the drums reached a crescendo, I started to feel decidedly anxious. Even at the finish the horses, sweating and pawing the ground, were too close for comfort and I was glad when the speeches were over and we were able to head for home and a cold drink.

\*\*\*

The following day we visited our American friends Kitty, Dick and Melissa, their two year old daughter, at KULP Bible and Farm School about ten miles north of Mubi at Mararaba. Dad described the visit in his diary: '*Before dinner we went round the mission farm with Dick who explained that they were teaching crop rotation. This consisted of first year guinea corn followed by cotton and ending with groundnuts. Many bush people only grow guinea corn and move off the ground when it is exhausted. We had Nigerian food which had been cooked traditionally over three hot stones in a locally made cooking pot.'*

Mum and Dad were surprised when our friends told them that they were only allowed to return to the USA on leave every three years.

'It goes back to the time before cheap air travel and, of course, the journey by sea is long.' explained Kitty wistfully.

'Have you taken your parents to Michika?' asked Dick, changing the subject. 'Roger was here this morning. I asked him to join us this evening but he said he had a meeting with the Chief and had to get back. And he didn't want to be driving his motorbike in the dark. But he said you should call and see him if you go to Michika.'

'Roger is translating the Bible into Higgi, the local language there. Maybe we could go tomorrow?' I looked at Adrian.

'Yes, let's. We could look round then take that road we saw going towards Finger Mountain.'

I nodded. The road was just a rough track but it had looked enticing when we drove past on our way back from visiting students on teaching practice in Michika.

***

The following morning we set off for our expedition into the mountains. As we neared Michika we passed a man cycling with a child on the crossbar and a goat strapped to the carrier. We parked under a mango tree near the market and wandered among the stalls selling hand woven blankets, cutlasses and other implements but we kept well away from the meat buzzing with flies.

We stopped outside Roger's house which was a small hut on the edge of the market but he wasn't in so we returned to the car and began our expedition into the mountains.

At first the track was compacted sand, snaking between a sea of honey coloured grass but as we ascended we found ourselves bumping over loose rocks. A mangy dog ran out from a collection of thatched huts barking furiously as it tried to keep up with our car. Ahead of us were the mountains with the ancient volcanic plug known as Finger Mountain rising like a huge phallic symbol in the distance

By now we were getting thirsty and started looking for a shady picnic spot. We stopped at a Christian mission house that appeared to have been unoccupied for some time. We pulled into the overgrown driveway, put up folding chairs in the shade of a lemon tree and brought out the cool box and water cooler. Mum and Dad were quite at ease as they speculated about the previous inhabitants but we felt as if we were trespassing and were happy to move on when we had finished our picnic.

Just past the mission house was a small village but that also appeared deserted. However, we realised why when we turned a corner and saw a wedding party. The bride and groom were being carried on chairs by a throng of people singing, dancing and waving umbrellas. We slowed to watch and shouted a greeting but the revellers were oblivious to us.

The road began to resemble a river bed as we forded a stream and then bumped up a steep incline. We passed a group of old men drinking burukutu, the local beer made from guinea corn. They stared at our car as we lurched forward, regardless of the fact that we were a long way from home in a vehicle with no four wheel drive. I glanced at Mum and could see she was enjoying every minute of it. Finally we came to a halt on the bank of a dried up river which we guessed was the border with Cameroon. In many ways it was a relief to get out of the car and know we had reached the end of our journey – for today at least.

Adrian negotiated a nifty turn around and we headed back. The old men were still drinking burukutu and they shouted at us to join them. By 'us' they meant Adrian and Dad but by this time they had been joined by a group of women and girls. A couple of the women were dressed in a similar fashion to the Gude 'leaf ladies' although, instead

25

of leaves, they wore a dagger-shaped leather apron hanging from their waist and a larger tassled apron behind.

A young woman in a traditional wrapper and headscarf had a baby on her back. When Mum smiled and pointed at the baby, the young woman's mother indicated proudly that it was her grandson. She looked at us and, in sign language, asked if we were mother and daughter. When we said yes she looked pointedly for signs of a baby and appeared to admonish me for not producing a grandchild. I laughed but Mum simply sighed as she looked longingly at the baby on the young woman's back. As we took our leave the older woman held my mother's hand as she bade her a warm farewell.

On the drive back I sensed Mum's disappointment. Adrian and I had been married nearly four years and I knew Mum thought it was time we produced a grandchild. 'After all, it's not as if you're in your early twenties,' she had said soon after she arrived then clapped her hands to her mouth and apologised.

*  *  *

The rest of Mum and Dad's time with us was spent shopping in the market, going on short excursions into the surrounding area and a flurry of visits to friends. Dad and Adrian also went on several bird watching trips with the Principal of the Secondary School.

Our final excursion was to the small border town of Maiha. We stopped for a picnic under a mahogany tree and watched a pair of sunbirds feasting on mistletoe flowers in the branches. On our return we were uneasy as we saw a fast moving wispy cloud formation and explained to Mum and Dad that it probably heralded the arrival of the Harmattan wind from the Sahara.

We had been right to be worried. The new term began the day before Mum and Dad were due to leave but I was given permission to take them to the airport in Maiduguri. We drove through thick Harmattan dust for the first half of journey. Their flight from Maiduguri was cancelled and the following morning I bundled them on a long distance bus to Kano. They missed their international flight but eventually arrived home safely with a wealth of memories to see them through the winter.

\*\*\*

I felt restless after Mum and Dad left and was pleased to have Scout Camp to occupy me a month later. All school clubs had a teacher as the Patron and I was happy to be Patron of the TTC Scouts; the role didn't involve much apart from attending the annual Scout camp.

Adrian and I followed the college lorry laden with Scouts and equipment to the base of Uba Mountain. The breast-shaped hill was made of volcanic rocks that looked as if they had been tipped there by some angry giant. Acacia trees and thorn bushes clung for a foothold in the thin soil between the rocks.

I stumbled as I got out of the car and felt a blast of heat. The Scouts were already hacking down branches and dried grass to make shelters for the night while we looked for a flat surface to erect our little two-man tent. Grit blew into my eyes as I attempted to help Adrian with the tent poles with the canvas flapping in the wind. The dust seemed to settle in my stomach and, after a meal of goat cooked in thick red palm oil, I began to feel decidedly queasy and spent a restless night.

We were woken at dawn by the Scouts eager to climb the mountain before the heat became too intense. I swallowed some warm orange juice, got dressed and peered out of the tent. The Harmattan had blown again in the night and the bushes and shrubs were covered in white dust.

'Good morning Mrs Rosser. How are you today?' Hassan, my favourite scout, was so full of enthusiasm that I gave a broad smile and assured him I was fine.

Adrian had already begun the ascent. There was no

path but that did not deter the Scouts who scampered about, delighted with the freedom of a weekend away from college. It was an entirely different matter for me and the climb was more of a scramble on all fours with my nose buried in the choking dust. About half way up I gave up.

Adrian came back down to find out what was wrong.

'I think I'm pregnant!' I whispered.

His face lit up with joy as he helped me down the mountain. After making sure I was comfortable in a patch of shade, Adrian went back to join the scouts, leaving me to contemplate the implications and practicalities of pregnancy in the Mandara Mountains.

A few days later I wrote to tell Mum and Dad that they were to become grandparents.

# Chapter 3   Ahmadu is suspicious

Melinda was born in England on United Nations Day.

The weekend before, Adrian had driven the one hundred and sixty miles to Maiduguri to make an international telephone call. He booked into Lake Chad Hotel and spent the entire weekend trying to get through to my parents' phone but he could not even get a line out of Nigeria. As soon as Melinda was born, Dad sent Adrian a telegram. It was delivered five days later.

Melinda was nearly six weeks old when we arrived in Mubi. I was touched by the number of students and colleagues, including the college Imam, who called to welcome myself and our daughter.

Three weeks after we arrived, Melinda celebrated her first Christmas. Adelchi and Clive, our friends at the secondary school, invited us along with our Canadian friends, Helen and Keith, for Christmas Day. I had brought presents from England for Adelchi and Clive's children and they gave me a beautifully woven cotton wrapper so that I could carry Melinda on my back in traditional African style.

It was only a ten minute drive back to our house but Melinda was tired and hungry. In our hurry to get her settled we forgot to lock the car; in fact we even left the keys in the ignition.

Accumulated exhaustion had crept up on us and we went to bed early but I was up a few hours later to feed Melinda. It took me a while to get back to sleep and I was startled when Adrian woke me at five o'clock.

'Did you hear that?' he asked and, clad only in his underpants, jumped out of bed.

I yawned as I registered the spluttering sound of a car attempting to start. I got up and peeked at Melinda in the next room. Mercifully she was still asleep as, by this time, I could hear Adrian shouting.

I hurried to the front door and watched in horror as our

car began to lurch towards Adrian who was brandishing a large stick. He leapt out of the way and the car came to a halt as two figures loomed out of the darkness. For a moment I thought the person in the car had accomplices and was relieved when I heard the familiar voices of Ahmadu and Yakubu who had rushed from the servants' quarter to see what was happening. Not wanting to leave Melinda on her own in the house I stood helplessly by the door as I tried to follow the mixture of English and Hausa. Our neighbours were away but the shouting attracted their houseboy and gardener who, anxious not to miss anything, joined Ahmadu and Yakubu as they attempted to drag the thief from the car.

'Stop!' Adrian called.

He pushed the boys out of the way and peered into the car. I could see the whites of the young man's eyes behind the steering wheel, wide with fear at the sight of the angry houseboys.

'Give me the keys,' Adrian said calmly.

The man bowed his head as Adrian slowly took the keys from the ignition. He held them up for me to see and raised his eyebrows enquiringly. Neither of us knew what to do.

'We must send for Police!' said Ahmadu.

'I will go.' Yakubu, our gardener, was older than the others and commanded respect.

This still left us with the problem of what to do with the thief although he did not appear a threat as he whimpered with his head on the steering wheel.

Streaks of light appeared above the Mandara in the east and I saw Ahmadu eyeing up the rope we had strung between two trees as a washing line.

'We must tie him up!' he said excitedly.

'I think it will be enough to lock the doors,' said Adrian and walked round the car, carefully locking each door. 'Now you stand guard till the police arrive. I must look after Mrs Rosser and our baby.'

'And get dressed,' I thought as I watched Adrian come

30

towards the house. When he reached the door his hand brushed against the Christmas decoration we had hung on the outside and a piece of silver tinsel fluttered to the ground.

Melinda was just waking up and playing with her cuddly white rabbit blissfully unaware of the drama outside. Her blue eyes lit up in recognition as I lifted her from her cot. I held her close, my heart still thumping, suddenly filled with the enormity of the responsibility of keeping her safe. I took her to our bedroom for her morning feed and Adrian, now dressed in shorts and T-shirt, brought two mugs of tea.

'I wonder how long it will take for the police to come,' I said feeling calmer now with Melinda nestled to me.

'I suppose it depends what else is going on and who's in charge.'

I nodded. We had met the Police Superintendent on several occasions at the Club and he had told us that he had done some of his training at the police college in Wakefield, England.

Adrian drained his cup. 'I'll go and keep an eye on things. I suggest you and Melinda stay this end of the house if possible.'

I changed Melinda's terry towel nappy and put it in the steriliser bucket in the bathroom. Then I snuggled down next to her and we both drifted off to sleep.

The ringing of a bicycle bell woke me and I looked out of the window to see a policeman cycling up our driveway. I quickly got dressed, put a pillow on either side of Melinda so she couldn't fall out of bed, slipped on my sandals and went outside.

Ahmadu and our neighbour's houseboys were still guarding the car and the policeman was writing in his notebook as Adrian explained what had happened. I wondered who the thief was and why he had attempted to steal our car when it was obvious he didn't know how to drive. He didn't appear to be a professional thief or even a joy rider although I had to admit I had no first-hand knowledge of either.

At the policeman's request Adrian unlocked the driver's door and wound down the window a fraction so that he could question the thief. Unfortunately the policeman was from the south of Nigeria and his Hausa wasn't fluent. In any case the man was too terrified to speak.

We had reached an impasse when Yakubu returned. 'They will send reinforcements later,' he announced.

I felt uneasy as I wondered what form this would take.

'Can you ask him why he tried to steal the car,' I said.

Yakubu spoke to the man in Hausa but received little response. He then changed to a language I recognised as Gude although I couldn't understand the conversation.

'What are they saying?' demanded the policeman.

'He says he needs to visit the family of his betrothed about the bride price,' said Ahmadu who had been listening intently.

'But why did he want to steal our car?' I asked.

'Their house is far.' Ahmadu pointed towards the mountains. 'And time is running out.'

I wondered if there was another suitor waiting who was able to offer the bride price. For a moment I forgot about the possible damage to our car and wished I knew more about the customs of the people we were living among.

The thief suddenly became agitated.

'He needs the latrine,' said Yakubu.

The policeman said he wasn't allowed out of the car but Adrian intervened, fearful of the consequences for our car if permission was refused. Yakubu and Ahmadu, followed by the policeman, led the man to the toilet in the servants' quarter. I went back into the house and checked on Melinda who was still sleeping.

When I returned outside everyone was walking quietly back from the toilet with the thief showing no signs of resistance. Suddenly there was a loud squawking and a guinea fowl flew straight towards them, its wings flapping noisily. Someone shrieked and pandemonium broke out.

The thief seized his opportunity and ran. As he passed me hovering by the door he stumbled and grabbed at the Christmas decoration festooned with silver tinsel.

Fearful for Melinda, I hurried into the house but, despite the shouting, she was still sleeping. I watched from the bedroom window as everyone stampeded past and tackled the unfortunate man in our front garden. Adrian attempted to calm everyone down but Ahmadu rushed to the washing line and came back with the rope. Encouraged by the policeman he and the other houseboys tied up the protesting man while Adrian looked on helplessly.

Melinda muttered at the sound of a siren but did not wake up. With a screech of brakes a police car came to a halt in our driveway. Gesturing to his driver to remain in the car, a police inspector got out and shook hands with Adrian. He then turned to the policeman.

I opened the window so I could hear what was said.

The thief let out a terrified cry as the inspector looked at him then glared at the houseboys standing triumphantly around him.

'Why is this man trussed up like a chicken?'

The houseboys looked confused and shuffled uncertainly.

'The man knows witchcraft, he is eating juju,' the policeman said importantly.

The inspector frowned and turned to Adrian. 'Do you know this man? Does he want to harm you?'

'No, I've never seen him before.'

'How do you know he is eating juju?' the inspector asked.

'You can see it in his mouth.' The policeman pointed to the figure on the ground.

I watched Adrian and the inspector bend down to take a closer look at the man and was surprised to hear Adrian laugh.

'Some people might call this juju but the silver in his mouth is tinsel from our Christmas decoration!'

He led the inspector to show him the decoration which

was now in tatters but still hanging from the door. The inspector was silent for a moment as he examined it.

'Haba!' he exclaimed and laughed as he shook hands with Adrian again.

The houseboys looked chastened as the Inspector spoke rapidly to them in Hausa and ordered the policeman to untie the prisoner.

We watched as he struggled with the vicious knots until Adrian handed over his penknife to speed things up.

By the time he was free the thief was shaking and made no resistance when he was handcuffed and taken away in the police car.

Ahmadu became quite a celebrity among the other house boys and we were the butt of jokes among our colleagues about our knowledge of making juju. A couple of months later we were summoned to appear as witnesses at the trial. We were shown into a room in the small court house. The formal proceedings were conducted by the magistrate, a dignified man wearing a white caftan and turban. Our thief received a fair hearing and was sentenced to three months in Mubi jail for attempted car theft.

\*\*\*

The rest of the holiday passed quickly preparing for the new term and sorting out Melinda's childcare. It had not been easy to find the right person. I wanted someone who could speak English and had experience of children. But women with good English generally had jobs and married Muslim women rarely worked outside the home.

Melinda enjoyed her walks when I took her in the pram around the TTC compound. All the houseboys and their wives wanted to greet the blonde baby who smiled and gurgled at everyone. I always stopped and chatted to an Igbo woman called Victoria. She was thin and had a nervous energy about her, gesticulating as she enthusiastically gave me tips on caring for my baby.

Victoria's husband, Isaac, had worked for our

colleague, Richard, when he was a teacher in Nigeria before the Civil War. When Richard got a post at the TTC he asked Isaac if he would like to work for him. Isaac was delighted to have the opportunity to work for his old boss again and so he and Victoria left war ravaged Eastern Nigeria and came to Mubi. They were considerably older than most of the other houseboys and their wives. Settling into the north east of Nigeria where the language, food and culture were different from their own could not have been easy for them. When Isaac came to see me after Christmas about his wife caring for my daughter he said in recommendation that she had borne ten children and eight had survived. She had an open warm hearted personality so I agreed to employ her as a nanny.

I went back to work eleven weeks after Melinda was born and I was barely recovered from a difficult birth let alone everything else. My parents had looked after me wonderfully, from the time I said goodbye to Adrian at the end of our annual leave in September to putting me on the plane at Gatwick three months later. To make up for Adrian's enforced absence, my mother made sure I had plenty of visitors, both during my week in hospital and at home. In fact, by the time I arrived in Nigeria with Melinda I was worn out with socialising, let alone travelling six thousand miles with a baby to live with a man I had not seen and rarely spoken to for three months.

Adrian and I had no experience of babies. The family support network which I had taken for granted at home simply did not exist for us here. I had assumed that the Principal's wife, an Englishwoman who I had worked with for the previous eighteen months, would be there to give me advice, as she had done throughout my pregnancy. However, she did not even visit me when I returned with Melinda or ask after her when we met at college almost every day. It was many years later that I realised she was probably too depressed by her own situation of having children at boarding school in England to want to help me; in fact my baby only served to remind her of what she no longer had.

Despite being constantly tired, I managed to be in the classroom at 7.15 with my lessons prepared and I gained energy from the friendly faces of my students who were pleased that I was back. Melinda always seemed happy with Victoria when we returned for the breakfast break at 9.15 and at the end of the college day at 1.15. She cared for her with enthusiasm, singing to her in English and Igbo. One day I found her sitting on the floor with one arm round Melinda who was propped beside her as she clapped her other hand on the floor shouting 'One, two, three!' in an effort to teach Melinda to count.

Her enthusiasm was infectious and I smiled as I said, 'She's too young for that.'

Victoria shook her head vigorously. 'Your baby is very clever, Madam.'

I was hardly aware of Ahmadu scowling as he put our breakfast on the table.

# Chapter 4    Birth of an idea

'Don't tell me you're taking the baby to Scout Camp!' The Principal's wife glared at me as I walked into the staff room.

'I could hardly leave her behind!' I retorted.

'But you have no business to be going!'

'Of course I do! I'm their Patron.'

I turned my back on her as I looked in my pigeon hole. 'No letters,' I muttered and left the room.

Hassan hurried towards me as I walked despondently across the college compound.

'Are you looking forward to camp, Madam? You will be very comfortable, the Chief has invited you and the Guides to sleep in his rest house.'

His enthusiasm was infectious. 'That will be lovely; I'm looking forward to it,' I said and realised that I was ready for my first trip out of Mubi since Melinda and I had arrived three months earlier.

\*\*\*

This year Melinda wasn't the only new girl as four of the female students were Girl Guides and had been given permission to attend the camp. Segregated accommodation had been arranged in Maiha, a village on the Cameroon border which was the venue for that year's camp.

Keeping at a safe distance in our Renault 12, we followed the lorry along a rutted dry season road that became impassable in the wet season. A few months later the explorer, Christina Dodwell, who we met when she was passing through Mubi, was to use this track when she travelled on horseback across the Mandara.

We pulled up behind the lorry outside Maiha primary school which consisted of single storey white-walled classrooms and an office-cum-store room on three sides of a square. Two of the older pupils welcomed us. This year

37

the Scouts were sleeping in a classroom so, unlike the year before, there was no rush to build shelters.

Isa, a village elder wearing a dark blue robe and turban, took us to the rest house. Pink periwinkle flowers gave a welcoming feel as we stepped into the compound. There was a two bedroom mud walled house, a latrine, a washroom and an area outside for cooking. This was luxury accommodation compared to the previous year.

Three of the Guides were torn by what they considered their duty to me as a first time mother versus their understandable desire to join the Scouting activities. The fourth Guide, however, had no qualms in appointing herself my helper for the weekend and the other girls gratefully left Melinda and I in the capable hands of Rebecca.

The eldest daughter of a pastor, Rebecca had a maturity beyond her eighteen years. She was intelligent and confident and we became good friends during the rest of our time in Nigeria.

When I was sitting comfortably in the shade of the house feeding Melinda, Rebecca announced that she was going to heat the water for my bath. I demurred that it was unnecessary and I would have a cold bath in the evening.

'But you are a first time mother,' she said. 'It is the custom for someone to bring hot water every morning and evening for you to wash yourself.'

I was touched by her kindness. But I was also aware of a gulf of understanding even in such a universal event as childbirth. I had heard of an Englishwoman who had been given boiling water to wash herself after giving birth in a Nigerian hospital. Still in pain and faced with a bowl of scalding water, she left it to cool but it was taken away and she was accused of being dirty.

In one corner of the compound was a huge pottery urn. Rebecca carefully took off the lid and filled an enamel jug with water which she poured into a three-legged black pot and placed on the fire. When the water had boiled she took it to the washing area which was screened by a fence of woven grass.

'I will look after Melinda while you have your bath.' Rebecca held out her arms.

'Let's change her nappy first,' I procrastinated, not wishing to move in the languid midday heat.

I was happy to hand over Melinda and wasn't surprised when Rebecca told me that she had five younger brothers.

'Your mother must miss you,' I said as I watched her deftly fold the clean nappy.

For a moment her face clouded. 'People say we are like sisters. But you will meet her. You must visit us in our village. You would like that wouldn't you, Melinda.' She tickled her gently and Melinda laughed.

Seeing that my daughter was in good hands I made my way to the washroom. The pot of water stood on a table next to a calabash which was used for scooping water over the body. It was an efficient system and the water drained away easily. Next to the washroom was a pit latrine which attracted some flies but served its purpose.

I emerged to find we had visitors. Two boys in immaculate shorts and T-shirts had come to look at the white baby and practise their English. Rebecca held Melinda on her knee like a prize exhibit and would not let the boys touch her.

Throughout the day a stream of well-dressed children of all ages arrived to see the baby and strike up a conversation with me. They were well mannered and confident although the little girls giggled behind their hands as I tried to draw them out. Finally an older boy came and told the children to leave us in peace. I had enjoyed their company but was glad of the opportunity to rest as, by now, it was very hot and I wanted to be refreshed for the evening activity.

Adrian and the three Guides arrived back in the late afternoon exhilarated from their day of tracking, stalking and collecting wood for the camp fire.

After everyone had bathed and changed we made our way to the Chief's compound where he was holding a durbar in our honour. Isa met us at the entrance and showed us to our seats on a wooden platform at the other end of the high-walled compound. The Scouts sat on the ground along the two facing walls. From somewhere outside we could hear snorts and whinnying accompanied by shouts as the horses were prepared.

Isa re-appeared with the Chief and we were formally introduced. He courteously enquired after the sleeping baby in my arms and congratulated Adrian on his firstborn. Adrian thanked him respectfully and asked how many children he had.

'Twenty-eight,' he replied gravely as he took his seat next to us.

We were slightly nonplussed and then I realised that the children who had visited us throughout the day were all his; I had thought that they had similar features and now I understood why.

Unlike the durbar we had witnessed in Mubi the previous year, there were only three horses in the line-up but the spectacle was just as terrifying as they charged straight towards us and slithered to a halt so close that we could feel their breath upon us. The horses' brightly coloured woollen bridles shook as the riders pulled their mounts to a standstill; then they turned and trotted back before making another charge.

Melinda woke up at the second charge, her eyes wide open in fear. The sound of her terrified scream was lost amid the thundering hooves and wild cheers from our Scouts. I wanted to take her away but there was no escape so I did the only thing I could and fed her, as if attending a durbar with my baby at my breast was a natural occurrence.

When it was over, the Chief had a word with Isa who hurried off. He returned later and gave something to the Chief who again congratulated us on our firstborn then presented me with a fan woven from brightly coloured wool to give to my daughter.

I thanked him but was pleased that the durbar was over

so that I could take Melinda back to the calm of the rest house.

Rebecca remained loyally at my side later when Adrian and the Guides left to spend the rest of the evening around the camp fire. I felt that I had had enough excitement for one day and elected to stay by our own fire listening to Rebecca's tales of growing up in her village.

\*\*\*

Back in Mubi I felt a sense of anti-climax. Lessons had to be prepared and we were coming up to the time when our fourth and fifth year students went on teaching practice. Helping my students plan their lessons and watching them teach eager children in often overcrowded classrooms was my favourite part of the job, especially when it involved me driving, often on my own, to schools in the villages. This year the Principal had ensured that all my visits were to schools within or very near Mubi. However, I was beginning to have reservations about whether I wanted to entrust Melinda to Victoria's care when I was away from the college compound.

As the term continued I became increasingly exhausted and was unable to see the underlying tension between Victoria and Ahmadu. Things came to a head when we came home for breakfast three weeks before the end of term.

On this particular morning Ahmadu was waiting for us in an excited state.

'That woman is abusing your daughter!' he declared.

He claimed that Victoria was beating her but there was no evidence of this. When confronted, Victoria vigorously denied the charge and proclaimed her love for Melinda.

Ahmadu would not expand and I felt in my gut that he was lying. I was never away from Melinda for more than three hours at a time and it was obvious that she was a happy baby and developing well. She rarely slept through the night but this was unsurprising as it was the hottest time of the year.

Rightly or wrongly we asked Victoria to leave immediately.

Adrian said he would let my classes know that I was unable to teach them for the rest of the day. When he came home at half past one we talked about how to resolve the child-care issue and decided to ask the Principal if I could work part-time after Easter. We did not want to rush into finding a replacement for Victoria so this left us with the immediate problem of how I would carry on teaching for the last three weeks of term. As it happened, our timetables gave us free periods at different times so we could just about manage to look after Melinda between us if the Principal agreed. There was a Government regulation that women were allowed to leave work an hour early for a year after childbirth. Up till then I had not taken advantage of this but I decided to suggest I used my daily hour to cover the times when we were both supposed to be teaching.

The Principal was usually in his office well before the four o'clock roll call and afternoon activities. Feeling confident with my proposed solution to our problem and slightly less weary, I left Melinda with Adrian and made my way past the other staff houses to the college. It was the hottest time of the year but several scarlet flamboyant trees in front of the administration block had burst into bud in expectation of the imminent rains.

Maliki, the art teacher, was standing at the Banda copying machine and the familiar smell of methylated spirit filled the room. As I greeted him I noticed that his hand was stained purple from the ink.

'Is it playing up again?' I asked sympathetically. I had spent my free period that morning copying some notes I had written for 4B the following day.

'I think there is juju in this machine!' He laughed ruefully.

'Excuse me.' Jonah, the assistant history teacher, looked up from his marking. 'Is this spelling correct?'

I sighed as I bent over yet another lesson plan on the slave trade triangle, a subject I had only scanty knowledge of when I first came to Nigeria but which seemed to be a favourite for teaching practice lessons.

'Caribbean has two Bs,' I said helpfully and made my way to a door at the end of the staff room.

The small office was crowded with several filing cabinets and a large desk covered in papers.

'Did you hear the World Service at lunch time? Mariner 10 has sent back pictures from Mercury,' the Principal said as I hovered by a chair piled with files.

'Oh.' My carefully prepared speech deserted me as I regarded the bluff, hardworking man from the north of England who had been my boss for the last couple of years. The problem was that in our small ex-pat community we had also been to each other's houses for dinner and for a while I had even been the recipient of his wife's confidences.

From outside I heard students talking as the college woke up from its afternoon quiet time. But my mind was re-playing the distressing scene in the morning as Victoria and I tussled for possession of Melinda followed by her shrieks as Adrian led her away.

'Is everything all right?' The man behind the desk regarded me not unkindly.

I blurted out what had happened and my solution to the problem.

The Principal picked up a pencil and studied it intently. Without looking at me, he said that he would accept my resignation from the end of term.

I gasped, unable to comprehend what he was saying.

'But what about my exam class?' A feeling of devastation began to sweep over me.

'You will be happier at home with your baby.'

'But what about the students?' I whispered as I felt the fight drain out of me.

'That's my problem.' The Principal continued to twiddle with his pencil.

43

I forced myself to broach the immediate problem of my teaching commitment to the end of term.

He agreed that, for the next three weeks, Adrian and I would spend the minimum of time in the classroom so that we could look after our daughter between us until I took over completely at the end of term. We both knew that this would sometimes mean one of us arriving late at changeover times and so I swallowed hard and thanked him.

Fortunately the staff room was empty when I shuffled out of the Principal's office.

I kept my eyes downcast as I made my way home but I was unable to avoid Hassan from 4B.

'Good afternoon Mrs Rosser. How is your baby?'

I tried to smile. 'She is well thank you.'

He looked at me curiously as I brushed my hand across the tears coursing down my cheeks.

'This dust gets in my eyes,' I said and hurried past him.

\*\*\*

The next morning I was at home with Melinda when Ahmadu knocked on the kitchen door. Hovering behind him was a young woman he introduced as his sister.

'I have brought a girl to look after your baby.'

The girl was nervous as I glared at Ahmadu. 'I am looking after my baby.'

He looked confused.

'If Victoria isn't good enough then I'll look after her myself.' I shut the door and went back into the house.

A pile of exercise books lay on the table. I idly flicked through, recognising the names and handwriting of each student.

'What am I going to do if I can't teach?' I wondered miserably.

That afternoon we visited Adelchi and Clive. Their children, four year old Helen and three year old Phillip, were happy to play with Melinda who had reached that delightful stage of being able to sit up but remain where she was put.

Clive was head of the English department and Adelchi gave home economics lessons to small groups of girls in their house. They listened sympathetically to our news. Clive couldn't understand our Principal's attitude and suggested I approached him again to see if we could come to some arrangement. But, since I had returned from maternity leave, the Principal's wife had made my position in the English department very difficult.

'Do you know, she still hasn't come to see Melinda,' I told our friends.

'But you've been back three months!' Adelchi looked at me in disbelief.

I shrugged. 'Maybe she doesn't like me.'

'That's no matter. In my culture it is tradition to pay our respects to the family when a baby is born.'

'It is in ours too,' I said although I knew there were no hard and fast rules.

Clive appeared lost in thought. 'So, what do you think you'll do?' he asked.

I found myself telling them about an idea that had been at the back of my mind since the time I had spent with Rebecca in Maiha and had realised how different the Nigerian attitudes to pregnancy and childbirth were from those in England. I thought I could use some of the research techniques I had acquired in my sociology degree to study pregnancy and childbirth customs in this part of Nigeria. I explained that, if I was to do it properly, I would need reliable interpreters and introductions to a range of people. Most importantly, I would be able to do most of it with Melinda in tow.

Adlechi thought it was an excellent idea and promised to see if any of the girls she taught would be interested in helping me.

As we drove home I felt more optimistic about the future and my new career as a researcher.

# Chapter 5    Pastor Johanna's dam

The next three weeks weren't easy with juggling looking after Melinda and teaching. I had little time to think about my plans for when I would no longer be going into college every day. Both Adrian and I were ready for a break when the holidays came.

Our Italian friends, who had been part of the team building the new road to Maiduguri, had moved to Jos. They invited us to spend Easter with them and, apart from our weekend with the Scouts, it was our first trip away with Melinda. We enjoyed the luxury of staying in a modern air conditioned flat but they weren't used to having a baby around and we decided, for the sake of our friendship, to cut our visit short.

On our way home we decided to call on our friends, Jill and Dave, who were teaching in Maiduguri. They were expecting their first child and staying at the Vom Christian Mission Hospital outside Jos.

We parked under the shade of a purple bougainvillea tree and made our way past several small buildings to a low white-washed building in the middle of a large compound.

The receptionist looked at Melinda in her push chair and explained that the mother and baby clinic was the other side of the compound.

When we said that we had come to see Mr and Mrs Headey she smiled.

'She had her baby last night. They are both doing well but you must not stay long. She is in Room Five,' she said and pointed along the corridor.

The door was open and Jill was sitting up in bed nursing Jemima. Melinda was thrilled when I lifted her out of her push chair to see the baby. Her blonde head bent towards Jemima's dark hair as she solemnly handed her a little green sleeping suit that used to be hers.

Dave shook our hands, obviously pleased that we had

come. When he said he had been with Jill the whole time I felt a pang that Adrian hadn't been able to share Melinda's birth as Dave had shared Jemima's. In fact Adrian seemed shocked by how exhausted they both were.

'I've brought you this,' I said and handed Jill my well-thumbed copy of Doctor Spock's Baby and Child Care.

'Thank you. I'm sure it will be very useful. I don't really know what I'm doing!'

'Neither did I.' I smiled ruefully.

A nurse bustled in and was surprised to see Melinda.

'These are our friends from Mubi,' said Jill.

'Mubi; you have come far.' She appeared impressed then turned her attention to Jemima who had fallen asleep. 'How is she feeding?'

'All right. I think.' Jill looked at me and shrugged.

'You must rest when the baby sleeps. You must be strong for your child.' She looked at us pointedly as she left the small room.

We talked for a few minutes but I could see that Jill was tired and Melinda was beginning to fidget.

'You must stay with us next time you come to Maiduguri,' said Jill.

'That would be lovely, as long as it's not too much trouble. But we'll go now and let you catch up on some sleep.' I bent down and kissed Jemima's tiny forehead.

'Thank you for coming.' Jill smiled and closed her eyes.

As Dave walked with us to our car he told us they had applied for a visa for Jill's sister to stay with them and look after Jemima when Jill went back to her teaching job.

'I hope everything works out for you,' I said.

'I'm sure it will. Don't forget to come and see us when you're in Maiduguri.'

'We will. It was lovely meeting Jemima.'

Adrian strapped Melinda in the car and I put her bottle filled with blackcurrant juice into her outstretched hands.

The passenger seat was hot as I got in and wound down the window.

'How long will you stay here?' asked Adrian.

'I'm not sure. There's no petrol in town so we'll have to wait till the next delivery. It's not a problem as we can stay here an extra day or two if necessary. But,' Dave looked at us with concern, 'Have you got enough for the journey?'

'Yes, we filled the tank and our two jerry cans yesterday. Our friends recommended a filling station they knew had fuel. Anyway, enjoy the break while you can,' Adrian said as he removed the towel he had put on the steering wheel to prevent it from becoming too hot to touch.

'I will. Safe journey and thank you for coming.'

'See you soon!' I called as I waved goodbye.

A small crowd had gathered outside the hospital entrance where women were squatting under a thatched shelter cooking food to sell to hospital visitors.

Ahead of us was a man on a bicycle with a very pregnant woman on the cross bar.

'I wonder how far they've come,' said Adrian.

'She must be very uncomfortable.'

I pondered the gulf between our experiences then smiled in surprise when the woman waved to us as we drove slowly past. I waved back then fell silent as the road began to wind through forest at the western edge of the Jos plateau.

'I think it was a good omen,' I said after a while.

'What was?'

'Seeing the pregnant woman on the bicycle and being with a new born baby. I expect I'll see a lot more when I start my research.'

Adrian slowed the car as we began our descent to the Bauchi Plain.

'Yes, it will be good to get to know people outside the ex-pat community.'

\*\*\*

We enjoyed the rest of the Easter holiday, pottering about

and going for walks with Melinda who greeted everyone with an enthusiastic smile.

The fifth form students were pleased to see me when I arrived to teach the Methodology of English Teaching class but it was only twice a week. Adrian had been given permission to stay at home to look after Melinda during those lessons. The students worked hard and I was pleased that they achieved good exam results.

However, most of the time it was only myself and Melinda at home and, by the second week of term, I felt my horizons closing in. There were a dozen staff houses on the TTC compound but, as I was the only one who wasn't working, I relied on Adrian for information about what was going on.

Melinda was a poor sleeper and, as a result, I was tired a lot of the time but I brightened up when Rebecca called after lessons one afternoon. She was enthusiastic when I explained my idea of learning about the local customs and she invited me to spend a day at her parents' house.

We arranged to go when Adrian was at an examiners' meeting at Yankari Game Reserve. He got a lift early on Sunday morning with Idris, the maths teacher, so that I had the car while he was away.

Rebecca arrived at my house a couple of hours later. She was wearing a brightly patterned traditional outfit which was the school uniform worn by the girls on Sundays. The skirt, or wrapper, consisted of two yards of cloth which wrapped around the waist, the blouse was made from the same cloth and the final piece of cloth was used either as a headscarf or to tie a baby on the back.

I felt a sense of anticipation as I drove out of the TTC compound and headed east towards Cameroon. It was the middle of May and the beginning of the rainy season. We had already had a couple of rains and the parched earth was transformed into a carpet of green. The dry season dust had been washed away and the mountain peaks were clearly visible, range upon range, straddling Nigeria and Cameroon. The air became cooler as we climbed out of the valley towards Sahuda.

As I drove, Rebecca told me about her family. Her father, from the Gude tribe, had trained as a pastor at Kulp Bible School. She was pleased when I said that I knew the place. Kitty and Dick had explained to us how families came for three years and were each given a plot of land to farm so that they were relatively self-sufficient. There was a school for the children and, as well as pastoral training and Bible study, students also followed a practical farming course. The idea was that, when the pastors and their families returned to their villages, they would use the farming methods they had learned and their example would encourage others to experiment with different crops and small-scale irrigation methods.

'My father is the best farmer in Sahuda,' Rebecca said proudly.

As we neared the village Rebecca wound down her window and shouted greetings to a woman with a baby on her back and a basket on her head.

'They'll be coming out of church now.' Rebecca looked animated as we turned off the road and parked on some rough ground near a small building with a cross on its tin roof.

The service had finished and Pastor Johanna was standing by the door chatting to people. Some of the men wore rigas, others crisply ironed shirts and trousers. Like Rebecca, the women were wearing their best wrappers and many had elaborate headscarves of the same material.

I held Melinda in the crook of my arm and she waved as Rebecca introduced us to her father. The pastor greeted us warmly and said that Hajara, his wife, was in a meeting but it would finish soon. Rebecca told me that the women's meeting was a time when they could ask each other advice about their problems, especially their relationships with their pagan neighbours. As she said this a couple of women wearing leaves around their waist stopped and stared at my blonde-haired child. I felt tension fizzing from Rebecca as she looked at the women. Then her father called a greeting to them in Gude and the atmosphere calmed. They replied and seemed about to strike up a conversation with me but were interrupted by squeals from two little boys who flung themselves at Rebecca.

'These are my brothers,' she said and introduced us. 'You must speak English!' she commanded as they hung back, suddenly shy.

The eldest child solemnly put out his hand. 'Good morning. How are you?'

'I am very well, thank you,' I replied.

'What is your baby's name?'

I bent down and gave him Melinda's hand as I told him her name.

'I will take her,' said Rebecca proprietarily.

'All right.' I had every confidence in Rebecca as she put Melinda on her hip.

'There is my mother!' she cried and we hurried to meet her.

I was surprised that the mother of six children looked so young although she must only have been in her early thirties. The welcome she gave me felt like a blessing after the tribulations of the last couple of months.

'Our compound is near the river, said Rebecca.

We walked slowly through the village, stopping every now and again to greet people. Melinda enjoyed the attention and smiled happily at everyone we met. Unlike Mubi, there were no defined streets and the mud-walled compounds were larger than those I had seen in the centre of Mubi. We stopped to greet a woman who was drawing water from a well. I watched as she pulled up the bucket of water and placed it carefully on a padded cloth ring on her head.

'Sahuda has eight wells,' Rebecca told me proudly.

'How many people live here?' I asked.

Rebecca consulted her mother. 'She thinks it is about one thousand. But that includes people like my two brothers who are away at secondary school.'

Melinda laughed and pointed as we walked past a goat standing on its hind legs to reach fresh leaves on a scraggy bush.

'We're here!' Rebecca said happily as we stopped at the thatched entrance porch to a large mud walled compound.

The earth floor of the compound was spotless but, even so, Rebecca put down a mat for Melinda to sit on; I was relieved that she had not yet learned to crawl. The children played with her and brought a rattle made from a gourd with beans inside and Hajara took me on a tour of the compound. There was a large hut for the parents and another for the children. This second hut had a small room for Rebecca with a bed instead of sleeping mats. Behind the parents' hut was a pit latrine with cornstalk fencing. The kitchen hut had a fire sunk into the floor and a stone table used for grinding corn and herbs.

Rebecca brought me a folding chair to sit on and a bowl of warm water to heat Melinda's bottle. While I was feeding her, Rebecca and her mother conferred about what food they should cook then Hajara called one of the boys to get some things from the granary. Leaning against the granary hut with its conical grass roof was a rickety ladder. The boy nimbly climbed the ladder and lifted up the roof then disappeared inside the grain store. Moments later he re-appeared with a basket of guinea corn and some bunches of green vegetables. He passed the basket to Rebecca, waved then, ignoring the ladder, leapt to the ground and gave a bow, causing Melinda to chuckle and clap her hands in delight.

I had just finished giving Melinda her bottle when the Pastor arrived. We had cups of sweet tea as we talked about my interest in pregnancy and childbirth customs. They told me a little about their own experiences as Christians and said that they would introduce me to people to talk to. About half the village were pagan and there were a slightly higher number of Christians than Muslims. The pastor was happy for me to meet pagans because he predicted that, with universal primary education, their religion would die out and he felt that it was important for the old traditions to be recorded.

'But now you must see my farm,' he said and I realised that this was something he was very proud of.

*** 

Rebecca tied Melinda securely on her back where she dozed comfortably in the afternoon sun.

Just outside the compound was a tall baobab tree with fruit which looked like small rugby balls dangling on the outermost edges. Pastor Johanna picked up one that had fallen and explained some of its many uses, particularly for medicine as it was rich in Vitamin C, but also for making bark cloth and rope.

We stopped to examine the recently planted guinea corn, maize and groundnuts which were all sprouting nicely.

'Now I will show you my dam,' the Pastor said proudly and led the way down a steep path to the river.

Spanning the river was a solid earth walled dam and I was impressed when Rebecca told me her father had made it himself so that he could irrigate his crops. He showed me his beds of sprouting leaves for making soup and his orchard of bananas, guava and mango trees. Finally there was cassava, like a mini-forest, which I knew was high in carbohydrate but of little nutritional value. However, unlike many subsistence farmers, by using irrigation the pastor had been able to supplement this ubiquitous crop and provide a balanced diet for his family.

Rebecca, Melinda and I sat in the shade while Pastor Johanna pulled up some weeds. Two children walked across the top of the dam balancing large bundles of sticks on their heads. The narrow bridge was strewn with debris that had come down the river but they were surefooted despite their bare feet. Melinda waved at them then pointed in delight at a lilac breasted roller with turquoise wing feathers flying across the water.

I was beginning to feel thirsty but the guavas were not yet ripe. I could see the Pastor looking at me as I began to wilt in the heat. He went over to one of the banana plants and pulled back the large leaves to reveal a hand of small, almost yellow bananas.

'For you and your husband,' he said as he presented them to me.

I was about to thank him then I remembered that my words would diminish the gift. Instead I smiled and bowed my head. 'I am looking forward to telling my husband about your dam; I know he will be very interested.'

The smell of groundnuts mixed with wood smoke and herbs wafted towards us on our return to the compound. Four chairs were arranged in a semi-circle around a mat on the ground. I was invited to sit down and was given an enamel plate. Hajara brought out a large pot of guinea corn and a smaller pot of leaf soup made from groundnut paste and put them on the mat. The children sat quietly by the food and passed round a bowl of water for everyone to wash their hands. Rebecca, holding Melinda, sat next to me and her parents took the other chairs. Then the Pastor said grace.

I watched as everyone took it in turns to scoop the dough-like guinea corn from the pot, knead it into a ball and use it to scoop up some leaf soup. Then I took my turn but the corn held its heat as it stuck to my fingers. I wasn't sure what to do and was impressed by Rebecca's dexterity even with a baby on her knee. She patiently showed me the technique and I began to get the hang of it especially as it tasted delicious.

Shadows were beginning to creep across the compound and as soon as the meal was finished we prepared to leave. The whole family accompanied us back to the car and, with many invitations to return again, they waved until we were out of sight.

\*\*\*

The atmosphere in the TTC staff compound felt strangely quiet for the next couple of days with a quarter of the teachers away at the conference in Yankari. When I wasn't looking after Melinda I made notes about my day with Rebecca's family and everything I had learnt. I really wished I could look at the photos I had taken on my little instamatic camera but, as they were colour slides, I would have to wait till we returned to England for them to be developed. However, Adrian's camera took black and white photos which he developed and printed himself in our bathroom.

I was showing Melinda some photos of herself when Idris's car turned into our drive. 'Daddy's home!' I cried as I scooped her up and ran outside.

'How was Yankari?' I asked later as we sat watching the sun go down.

'There wasn't much time for sight-seeing but we relaxed in the hot pools and I took a few photos of elephants.'

Adrian wanted to know all about my trip to Sahuda and, energised by my visit, I told him about how the things I had seen were all fascinating background to my research project.

# Chapter 6    Chief Ardo's mountain

The following day I went to see Jim Wade who, as well as being the deputy principal, was a geography teacher with a keen interest in anthropology. He had lived in Mubi for almost ten years and had become something of an authority on the Fali tribe. They were close cousins of the Gude and shared many of the same traditions.

At first Jim was wary about my research but when he realised I wasn't going to tread on his toes he was helpful.

'This is such a remote area that there's very little written about it,' he said.

Jim introduced me to Marcus and Ahmed, two third year Gude students whose families lived locally. We agreed to visit Marcus's home village of Lamurde the following Sunday. Marcus said that he would send word to his parents about our visit and see if they could arrange for us to meet Chief Ardo who lived on Lamurde Mountain.

Until their fourth year, TTC students, whatever their age, wore white shorts. However all students were allowed to wear long trousers on Sundays and when they went outside the college compound. Marcus and Ahmed looked older and very smart in their white uniforms and green hats when they presented themselves at our house. Armed with my notebook and camera, I drove out of Mubi and along a bush road to Lamurde. This was not my first visit to the village as I had been to the primary school there on several occasions when I was observing students on teaching practice.

Marcus suggested that, before visiting the traditional chief, we should call on the government chief appointed by the local authority. I was intrigued that there were two chiefs and looked forward to finding out more. I drove slowly past the school and along what passed as the main street; taking care to avoid chickens, goats and children. We stopped at a house near the small mosque. There was a door made of corrugated sheeting in the centre of a mud brick wall. It was ajar and Marcus gave a gentle tap and clapped his hands. A woman with a baby on her back appeared and, after the greetings, pointed along the road.

'He is at the end of the street,' said Marcus as he returned to the car.

'Right,' I replied and, with my hands slithering on the hot steering wheel, edged forward.

'I can see him. Stop here.' Ahmed pointed to a white robed man walking in our direction.

We got out of the car and exchanged greetings. It took some time to explain my presence but eventually we all shook hands and it appeared I had been given permission to wander freely in the village but I should be careful of snakes on the mountain.

'Where shall we leave the car?' I asked, looking ahead at the rapidly deteriorating road.

'Outside my parents' compound. It is not far.'

We stopped outside a large compound surrounded by a high euphorbia hedge with sharp spikes.

'They have gone to market,' Marcus said after looking round quickly.

I caught a glimpse of pots waiting to be fired, half-finished pestles and mortars and a pile of wood shavings. It was bigger than Pastor Johanna's neat compound and appeared to be a place of work as well as a home.

'We will visit another time.' Marcus began to lead the way up a rocky track.

About half way up we came to a collection of huts.

'This is Lamurde Wamngo, the old village.' Marcus paused and shouted a greeting.

An old man was sitting on the ground outside one of the huts. A conversation ensued about the purpose of our visit and I realised it would have been impossible to wander up the mountain without a guide. Some children hovered nearby watching us with undisguised curiosity. The man beckoned to one of the boys and spoke rapidly, nodding in our direction.

'He has told the boy to guide us to the Chief,' said

Ahmed as we resumed our ascent.

Chief Ardo's compound was the highest dwelling place on the mountain. As we approached we saw that the roof of one of the huts had been newly thatched. At the pinnacle was a pottery finial rising above the golden straw. Most huts had a triangular metal cap covering the apex of the roof but this was intricately patterned and had obviously been made for an important person. Marcus said that the finial was on the hut belonging to the Chief's first wife. Laughing, he told me that, if the wife fell out of favour, her husband could remove the finial and place it on the favourite wife's hut.

On hearing our voices, a man wearing an indigo robe and embroidered hat appeared and said that he was the Chief's emissary. He recognised Marcus who introduced me and explained the purpose of our visit.

The emissary invited us to sit on a gravelled area below a huge flat rock opposite the compound while he informed the Chief about our visit. After a short time he re-appeared with a coloured blanket, climbed onto the rock and placed the blanket under a tree that was growing through a crack in the rock. Next to it were several hollows and a number of fist-sized grinding stones. The emissary explained that it was the custom for the Chief to be higher than his subjects and that he would see us when he was ready.

Chief Ardo emerged some time later wearing a white robe over another of indigo. A large pink scarf was wrapped turban style around his head and over his shoulder. It was not until he was sitting on the rock above us that he spoke, although at first he looked straight ahead rather than at us.

He asked what things I wanted to know and I told him that, since the birth of my first child, I wanted to understand some of the pregnancy and childbirth customs in this part of Nigeria. I also said that I would like to know something about the history of the tribe.

With Marcus and Ahmed interpreting, he told me that the Gude people originally came from the north but they were chased south by Fulani warriors who settled in what is now Mubi. The Gude divided into three clans, settling on hilltops at Lamurde, Sahuda and Gella where they felt protected from the Fulani. For many years a succession of paramount chiefs ruled over the tribe but in recent years the Government had appointed local chiefs.

Reading between the lines, I guessed that nowadays Chief Ardo's authority extended not much further than Lamurde Wamngo. I asked what his job entailed and he said that people came to him to settle disputes and for medicine. He gestured to the grinding stones and explained that he dispensed herbal remedies for stomach upsets, fevers and mental disorders. However, if I was interested in traditional medicine I should visit Awo, the witchdoctor.

He then asked if I would like to see the grave of Dawa, a great hunter who had founded the line at Lamurde when lions and elephants still roamed the land. I looked at Marcus and Ahmed. It was past noon and time to be getting back. There was some discussion and it was agreed that we would return the following Sunday

The walk back to the car was surprisingly quick. I had a lot to think about as I drove slowly home. And I had a dilemma. I had been spurred on to do the research to give me an interest while everyone else was teaching. However, in order to do it properly, I needed interpreters and the students were only available on Sundays.

As we rarely had pressing engagements on Sundays, the problem was easily solved.

\*\*\*

Adrian, Melinda, Marcus, Ahmed and I returned to Lamurde the next Sunday. We parked outside Marcus's compound and took the track to Chief Ardo's house. As before, his emissary waited with us at the meeting place until Ardo was ready.

On this occasion the Chief was wearing a simple white

caftan and red hat that fitted close to his head.

Adrian was introduced and greeted warmly but it was our daughter who stole the show as she laughed happily from the comfort of her sling on Adrian's hip.

As we began the ascent Ardo explained that he farmed most of that side of the mountain. The path became narrower and wound through what seemed like a forest of guinea corn, some of which stood higher than my shoulder.

Once we reached the top we stood respectfully by a cairn of stones. Ardo removed some of the top ones to reveal a grey phallus-shaped stone which he said was Dawa, the hunter and founder of his lineage. I murmured something reverential and then turned to look at the view.

I had thought we were on top of the world as I struggled to reach the summit but ahead of us the peaks rose higher. In the other direction I could make out Mubi in the centre of the meandering valley of the Yedseram River with the Mandara Mountains continuing beyond as far as the eye could see.

For a moment I felt in harmony with the vastness of Africa and with her secrets hidden within the ancient rocks. I looked at Melinda to see what she made of it all but she had fallen asleep nestled into the sling on her father's hip.

We turned and walked back the way we had come. The Chief came with us as far as Lamurde Wamngo and said that he would like to introduce us to his friend Awo, the witchdoctor. We came to a halt by a ramshackle collection of thatched huts clinging to a rocky outcrop at the side of the track. The Chief held up his hand indicating that we should wait while he went inside. While we were waiting Ahmed explained that, according to Gude tradition, only blacksmiths could be witchdoctors. Whereas Chief Ardo was a herbalist able to cure people of various ailments, Awo also practised divination and people visited him to foretell their future.

Melinda was still sleeping when we were beckoned into

the compound and introduced to the witchdoctor. He was sitting on the ground with his back to the wall of one of the huts. He wore a ragged shirt and loin cloth but his embroidered hat was perched at a jaunty angle and his eyes were bright. It was difficult to tell his age. He studied us intently as Chief Ardo introduced us and explained the purpose of our visit. Two young women sitting nearby pointed at Melinda and whispered to each other while Adrian and I smiled and nodded in our effort to communicate.

'He says he would like to tell you about some of our Gude traditions,' said Marcus. 'It is important they are not lost. We must send word and come another time.'

'Please tell him we look forward to that very much,' I replied as we took our leave.

Once outside the compound we thanked the Chief, and continued down the mountain to visit Marcus's family.

***

As we walked down the track Ahmed told me that Marcus's father was also a blacksmith but he did not practise medicine. I already knew that blacksmiths' families were regarded with a mixture of respect and suspicion. Many people considered blacksmiths unclean and not fit to eat with non-blacksmiths. However they also knew that without blacksmiths they would have no metal tools or items made of wood and without blacksmiths' wives there would be no pots.

When we entered the compound we saw Marcus's father busy at a large rock that served as a table on which were laid several freshly carved wooden hoe handles and an equal number of metal hoes.

He greeted us and called to his wife who was squatting on the ground polishing one of the pots I had noticed the previous week. She did not get up and Marcus explained that she was at a crucial stage with the glazing. Next to her was a girl of about seven and beside her were a couple of small misshapen pots. We exchanged greetings and the little girl pointed to her pots and talked rapidly to Marcus.

He laughed. 'My sister says she is learning to make pots and she plans to sell them in the market when our mother goes next time.'

As well as the cooking pots his mother was glazing, I noticed a couple of huge water containers.

'They must be difficult to transport,' I said.

'My senior brother has a donkey. His family also live here.' Marcus gestured to an inner compound behind a wall which had clothes hanging over it to dry.

'Please sit down,' he said, indicating a wooden bench in the shade. 'What questions would you like to ask?' he continued.

I would like to have asked his mother about childbirth but, in this mainly male company it did not seem appropriate. 'I would like to know how your mother makes her pots,' I said instead.

There was some discussion between mother and son.

'You should come when my mother is moulding the pots and she will explain everything. She will send word when she is ready.'

Melinda whimpered and opened her eyes. Adrian took her out of the sling and I gave her a bottle of juice. She drank thirstily then looked around and pointed at a hen with some chicks scratching in the dust. She laughed in delight and threw her sunhat on the ground.

Marcus's mother gazed at Melinda's straight blonde hair in amazement and his little sister edged forward to pick up Melinda's hat. As she handed it to me she asked a question.

'She wants to know if her hair will always be like that,' said Marcus.

I explained that it may get darker when we were in England away from the hot sun.

We felt very much at home as we sat quietly while Marcus's parents continued their work and his sister appeared to be questioning Marcus about the visitors he had brought. She looked at us in awe when he pointed towards the mountain and I realised what a privilege it had been to accompany Chief Ardo to the sacred burial place of the founder of his clan.

Suddenly the sky clouded over and a wind rippled round the compound, billowing the brightly coloured clothes hanging to dry.

'I think we should be getting back,' I said.

Marcus's parents did not press us to stay but said they looked forward to seeing us another time.

In the event, that was not for another four months because Melinda contracted measles soon after our visit. She was not desperately ill but it left us shaken and we were pleased to be returning to England on our annual leave.

# Chapter 7    Time out on Watership Down

Our home for the summer was a twelve foot Sprite Alpine caravan idyllically situated on chalk downland near Adrian's parents in Hampshire. Melinda thrived and, much to the delight of her grandparents, was walking by the time she was ten months old.

In some ways, our simple life near Watership Down was a bridge between the familiar world we knew and the very different world we had glimpsed when we went into the villages of the Mandara Mountains. However, although I could pretend our simple lifestyle gave me insight into life in a Gude village, there were no real comparisons. When I wanted to cook, I simply turned on the bottled gas. We used Melinda's baby buggy to carry water from the farmyard tap at the bottom of the hill to our caravan. We had a chemical toilet although no shower so bathed Melinda in warm water in a plastic bowl in the awning attached to the side of the caravan.

Regular baths were available when we hitched the caravan to our Vauxhall Victor and trundled off to visit friends and family. Melinda enjoyed meeting aunts, uncles, cousins, second cousins, great-aunts and children of various friends. My godmother, Barbara Pitt, was particularly interested in hearing about how life in Nigeria had changed since she was there.

Living in the open for a lot of that summer cleared my head and enabled me to consider how to continue my research on our return. Although I had studied research methods in my degree, I thought it would be helpful to have a sounding board away from the situation and so I enlisted the help of my brother, Nigel, who was studying Sociology. We talked about my research so far and Nigel recommended some books. He even set up a meeting for me with one of his tutors. She was enthusiastic about the project but I came away feeling I did not want to fit my research into a theoretical model. However, it was good to talk to people who understood about empirical research.

I asked Nigel to keep my letters which I wrote instead of a diary. In his replies he sometimes asked for clarification which was helpful because it made me look more closely at things I had taken for granted. The postal service between Mubi and London was generally reliable and things rarely went astray.

Apart from clothes for Melinda, her car safety harness and slide films, my most useful purchase that summer was a set of index cards for keeping records of everyone I interviewed. I later used this information to make a table with the names of the informants, where they lived, their occupation, religion and number of children they had.

While we were in England news of a coup in Nigeria was reported in the British media. It occurred when General Gowon was attending a conference of the Organisation of African Unity in Uganda and was called the Bloodless Coup as no lives had been lost in the takeover. Brigadier Murtala Muhammed was made Head of State on July 30th 1975 and was promoted to General. Brigadier Obasanjo became his Deputy.

Some of our relatives asked if we planned to return under the circumstances but we had no qualms about going back especially as Mubi was isolated from the main political centres. We promised to write to my parents as soon as we got back and were able to report that General Murtala Muhammed was a popular leader who was determined to root out corruption.

Sadly not everyone agreed with his policies and only eight months after taking power he was assassinated.

# Chapter 8    A wedding in Sahuda

On our return to Nigeria, we were pleased to find life in Mubi continuing as if the coup had never happened.

It felt strange being at home with Melinda when Adrian and my former colleagues were in their classrooms by 7.15. Unlike the previous term when I went in twice a week to teach my exam class, I had no reason to be on the college site. The easy communication I had enjoyed with the students and staff as I walked from the teachers' compound to the classrooms or staffroom had disappeared and I missed the comradeship.

I was eager to arrange another visit to Lamurde with Marcus and Ahmed and I particularly wanted to see Rebecca. However, college life was regimented and some of my colleagues were wary about what I was doing so I knew I had to tread carefully.

In the meantime, an Irish couple with their daughter, Gail, who was the same age as Melinda, had moved into the house next door. Although we had little in common apart from our children, I believe our almost daily contact relieved the monotony of our situation as non-working wives in a remote corner of Africa. Before Melinda was born my afternoons were relaxed; reading, writing letters or planning lessons. Children however, always seem to be full of energy. Gail's mother and I would huddle in a patch of shade by the side of one of our bungalows while our toddlers ran around regardless of the heat. Gail was rather unsure of our pet monkey but Melinda would happily let him groom her short blonde hair.

During any spare bits of time I transferred the interview notes I had made onto the index cards I had brought from England and planned how best to continue my research.

One of the people I had interviewed the previous term was Mr Dauda, a messenger working for the Local Authority. I was introduced to him by Musa, a young history teacher who had recently qualified at Ahmadu

Bello University. He accompanied Mr Dauda to my house at the end of the working day. Whereas Musa was casually dressed in a check shirt and slacks, Mr Dauda wore a long white robe and a white turban. He was a Muslim and seemed happy to talk to me about local customs. He told me that he had two wives, three sons and two daughters. He said that his sons were more important because the girls would go away after they married and that everything they had belonged to their husbands. Mr Dauda explained that Islamic law commands a groom to give his bride a gift before the marriage ceremony. This is different from the traditional meaning of bride-price in that it is given to the wife and not to the family of the bride.

I knew that bride price was a complex subject and I hoped to find out more on my next visit to Sahuda. Rebecca was keen to accompany me although she had less time now she was in the fifth form and working hard for her final exams.

*** 

We had been back three weeks when Rebecca and I paid a visit to Sahuda.

'Have you been to a Nigerian wedding?' Rebecca asked as we drove out of Mubi.

'We went to the bank manager's wedding last year but I'm afraid I disgraced myself.'

'What did you do?' Rebecca looked at me wide eyed.

'It was a mistake to wear my platform shoes especially as I was pregnant,' I paused for a moment as I remembered my delight at being a couple of inches taller in a shoe that appeared sensible as well as stylish. 'Anyway, there weren't enough chairs and we were standing for ages during the speeches. I must admit I felt rather sorry for both the wives,' I reflected as I recalled the two women dressed in identical peacock blue wrappers and elaborate headscarves sitting motionless in front of the guests who were becoming increasingly rowdy as the alcohol flowed.

Rebecca sniffed. 'These rich men like to show off by taking another wife!'

I remembered that there had been some disquiet about the wedding among the ex-pat community as we understood that the bank manager was a Christian.

I braked and swerved to avoid a pot hole. 'To be honest, the wedding was rather boring. It was dark and there were only a few tilley lamps so we thought we could creep away without being seen.'

'And did you?'

I laughed. 'The compound was gravelled and Adrian held my hand but I slipped and fell over pulling him down too. It made quite a crash!'

'Habà!' Rebecca exclaimed. 'Did you hurt yourself? You could have miscarried.'

'I was a bit shaken but more embarrassed than anything.'

As I concentrated on the road ahead I realised I was still embarrassed by the incident. Barclays Bank might only have been housed in a rudimentary building near the market but the Manager was an important person and it was an honour to have been invited to his wedding party. I knew I had offended custom by attempting to leave, even though Nigerian speeches are notoriously long and the seating arrangements often inadequate.

'It must have been difficult being pregnant without your mother near. It was good you went home to deliver.' Rebecca tactfully changed the subject.

I nodded. 'It was the way things worked out with our leave. But it wasn't easy being unable to share everything with Adrian.'

'It is important for the father to hold his new born baby.' Rebecca looked pensive and we drove in silence. 'Tell me about your wedding,' she asked after a while.

So I described my wedding in Weybridge parish church and how we stopped the traffic afterwards as we walked across the High Street for our DIY reception in the town hall. Eager for details, Rebecca questioned me about what I wore, who attended and the food we served.

'And what about your dowry?'

'My dowry?'

'The things you are given before you marry to keep you in your life as a married woman.'

'Well,' I hesitated. I knew it used to be the custom for young women to collect things for their bottom drawer but no one I knew had one. 'We have a wedding list of things we need so our friends and relatives can choose what they want to give us.'

'What gifts did they bring?'

I thought for a while. 'My parents gave us a dinner service and Adrian's a canteen of cutlery.'

Rebecca looked puzzled and so I explained what they were, feeling slightly wistful as I thought of them packed away in my parents' loft.

'Did you receive blankets?' she asked.

'Yes, and sheets. We brought them with us.'

'And cooking pots?'

'A few but they were too heavy to pack so we bought some in the market when we arrived.'

'I think there is a wedding in my village today. You will be able to see the custom here.'

'Will your father be officiating?'

Rebecca shook her head. 'They are Muslim but they also keep the Pagan customs. You will find it interesting.'

When we arrived at Sahuda she guided me past several compounds and we parked near a well where a woman was drawing water. Rebecca greeted her in Gude and asked a question. The woman shook her head and spoke rapidly, smiling and gesticulating as she replied.

'The bride has already left her parents' house. But people are there to see the dowry. We can join them.'

She led me to a compound surrounded by a cornstalk fence. 'Koko' she said as she clapped her hands at the entrance to announce our arrival.

We were greeted by an elderly woman who took us to a

table piled high with gifts. A group of women were having an animated discussion about the items. I looked in amazement at the stacks of brightly coloured enamel pots, thick cotton blankets, mats woven from grass, several large bowls of guinea corn and baskets of leaves. The sheer quantity made my own wedding gifts seem miserly in comparison.

'The bride is the only daughter,' said Rebecca seeing the expression on my face. 'Her mother has been buying these things for several years.'

The elderly woman asked Rebecca a question and nodded approvingly at my java print skirt.

'She wants to know if you are married.' Rebecca spoke rapidly to the woman who took my hands in hers and smiled approvingly.

I wasn't sure what to do when the other women turned their scrutiny from the dowry to myself. Rebecca explained who I was and about my interest in local customs.

'I'll tell you what they are saying later,' she whispered as a conversation ensued about the bride and groom. Then she thanked them and we took our leave.

'Your car will be safe here,' she said as we walked past it on our way to her parents' house.

'Do the bride's relatives give presents as well?' I asked.

'Three months before the marriage her future husband brought cloth from Mubi and had discussions with the father about the bride price. He brought the sum agreed two weeks ago and the Imam was called to celebrate the marriage.'

'Did it take place in the mosque?'

'Muslim women aren't allowed inside the mosque. It is different from our Christian marriage. The bride must stay inside her mother's hut while the male relatives gather in the compound and the Imam reads from the Quran and says they are joined in the name of the Prophet Mohammed.'

'Then what happens?' I asked.

'It is tradition that the bride runs to a friend and hides. That's where she is now. She will stay there all day until some of her older relatives find her and carry her away while she screams that she doesn't want to be married. They will take her to a hut and rub oil all over her body. After three days she will be carried to her husband's house where she'll spend the night on a sleeping mat with an old woman. The next day there is lots of singing and dancing as her goods, the ones we have just seen, are brought to her by her relatives.'

By this time I was beginning to think that my wedding had been very tame.

'And then what happens?'

'The things are unpacked, a ram is slaughtered and cooked and there is dancing all day and through the night. Two of the bride's friends stay for another three days preparing everything until the husband gives them money and they leave so the marriage can be consummated.'

'It all seems rather public,' I ventured.

Rebecca laughed. 'If the girl is a virgin there is special food cooked by the bride's grandmother and distributed to the neighbours. And her husband gives her cost money, maybe one hundred naira, but if she isn't a virgin she just gets one kobo!'

From what I had heard, virginity was an increasingly rare commodity but I made no comment.

Rebecca suddenly looked serious. 'These are traditional customs. They are not practised by Christians.'

I glanced up at the ancient volcanic peak rising above the village and felt a sense of alienation. And a very long way from home.

\*\*\*

A childish shout broke my mood and I laughed as two small boys ran towards us calling their sister's name. As before, I felt genuinely welcome when we reached the family's compound but this time I also had a comfortable

71

sense of familiarity.

'Did you have an interesting visit?' asked Pastor Johanna as we were eating our meal of guinea corn with okra and dried fish.

'I was sorry we didn't meet the bride but it was fascinating to see all her gifts and Rebecca told me about the marriage customs.'

'In this area they often mix the Muslim and Pagan traditions,' he replied.

'What happens at Christian weddings?'

Rebecca answered. 'If a boy sees a girl he likes he tells his father to see her father. If they agree to the marriage the boy's father will visit again and, if both families agree, they exchange kola nuts as a symbol of friendship between the families.'

'I am waiting for such a visit but not until my daughter has finished her schooling,' said the Pastor with a twinkle in his eye.

Rebecca was silent so her father continued, 'When the engagement is agreed the bride's father slaughters a ram and calls his and the groom's close relatives and also the Pastor to bless the engagement. After that they begin discussions about the bride price but the actual price is agreed only a few months before marriage.'

I didn't like to ask the monetary value of the bride price. As their only daughter who was training to be a teacher, Rebecca could probably command a high value but being Christians I guessed that her parents were slightly ambivalent about it.

'I was telling Rebecca about my wedding,' I said instead.

'You didn't tell me about your bachelor night,' she said.

I looked puzzled. 'Some women have a hen party the week before the wedding and the men have a stag party; is that what you mean?'

'The bachelor party happens the night before the wedding. All the bride's friends are invited to the bachelor night in the house of a friend of the groom. They dance till dawn while the groom spends a quiet evening with just a few friends. The next morning the bride's friends help her dress and they go by car to church for the marriage service.'

'Is there a party afterwards?'

'Of course. When the party is over some friends of the bride remain with her for a few days before it is time for her to be left alone with her husband.'

Rebecca's mother gestured that I should take more food but I was having trouble with the fish bones and declined politely.

'Do the Gude have any other marriage customs?' I asked.

'For Christians, it is tradition that the bride must not visit her parents' home or other relatives for three months. Muslims have the same tradition but they cannot return home for one year after the marriage.'

'But many traditions are dying out,' said the Pastor. 'It is good that you are recording them.'

I felt pleased. Even though I had started the research to give me something to occupy my mind it was good to know that it could be a useful record of a way of life that would probably change fundamentally within a generation.

We left shortly afterwards and Pastor Johanna walked with us to the car. 'You must bring your husband next time,' he said as he shook my hand.

# Chapter 9    Pregnancy and childbirth customs

A few days after my visit to Sahuda, Adelchi introduced me to two students at the secondary school who were interested in helping me with my research. They were friendly, intelligent girls and I arranged to pick them up after school the following day.

Melinda was excited about being looked after by Adelchi and ran off to play with Helen and Philip as soon as we arrived at their house. Hannatu and Hajara, wearing their Sunday wrappers, were waiting in the sitting room. They were attractive girls with their hair plaited in neat braids close to the scalp. Hannatu's skin was almost bronze while Hajara's was darker and she had striking black eye lashes. She told me that her father was a clerk with the Ministry of Agriculture and her mother cooked for the primary school next door to their house.

We drove to an area of new houses on the outskirts of Mubi and parked outside Hajara's compound. The house was a modern rectangular building made of cement blocks and with a corrugated iron roof. Hajara's mother, Sadaatu, greeted us at the door and we removed our sandals. She showed us into the living room which had family photographs on the white washed walls and motioned me to a comfortable armchair. Hajara and Hannatu sat on the two seater settee but Sadaatu squatted on a low stool, leaving the other armchair free.

Hajara explained that I was a teacher from England and had some questions to ask about pregnancy and childbirth customs. Sadaatu was unsmiling as she sat with her hands folded and I wondered if Hajara had let her know we were coming. However, when I explained that my baby had been born in England and I had brought her to Nigeria in an aeroplane when she was only five weeks old Sadaatu let out a startled 'Habà!' and asked her daughter how that was possible and where was the baby now. By the time we had established that Melinda was fine Saddatu began to relax and we got talking about morning sickness which I had suffered badly from when I was pregnant. Sadaatu nodded sympathetically and spoke rapidly to Hajara who translated that her mother had taken tamarind water in the first few months of her pregnancies.

I was asking her where she got the tamarind water when Hajara's father arrived home from work. He seemed surprised to see us but greeted me politely then settled in his armchair with a newspaper. He did not appear very interested in 'women's talk' and his presence may have influenced some of his wife's answers.

Unlike some of the people I had spoken to in Sahuda, she told me that the first person a woman tells when she discovers she is pregnant is her husband. Similarly, in answer to my question about what preparations are made for the baby, Sadaatu said that the husband buys soap and clothes for the mother and her baby. When I asked if pregnant women did any special exercises she said that pounding guinea corn keeps them strong. The family are Muslim and so Sadaatu said she didn't say any special prayers during pregnancy but she thought that people of other religions did.

Hajara and Hannatu conferred before translating my question about taboos during pregnancy and I wondered if it had been all right to ask this question. However, Sadaatu answered calmly that she had never observed any taboos but she had heard that some women who believed in these things were forbidden to take a bath in a flowing river because spirits could enter their womb.

We then went on to talk about where children are born. Hajara was the eldest of five children and the only one who had not been born in Mubi hospital but her cousins in the villages had all been born at home. In answer to my question about where the mother goes when labour begins Sadaatu said that the child chooses where it wants to be born. The mother may wish to deliver in the living room but some children prefer to be born outside or near the toilet and nothing can be done about it because it is God's will. She spoke rapidly to her daughter who frowned and was reluctant to translate.

'Hajara was born in the rainy season,' Hannatu explained. 'It was a cold night and so she wanted to be born in the kitchen because it was warm. It was before they moved to this house.'

I nodded, thinking that it made sense but the kitchen would have been smoky from the wood fire on the earth floor especially as there would not have been a chimney. I thought of the pristine delivery ward at St Peter's Hospital and the officious midwife in attendance at Melinda's birth and asked what help Sadaatu had when Hajara was born.

She leant forward, cupping her hands as she explained that the mother sits on a low stool supported by the village midwife or old woman and the baby comes out of its own accord. The midwife or helper sprinkles cold water on the baby to make it cry and the cord is tied and cut with a razor or sharp cornstalk. Unlike some women I spoke to later, Sadaatu said that the mother does not hold her baby until after her milk comes; in the meantime she is given some meat to eat and porridge to drink and the baby is cared for by the grandmother or other older relative.

'Is it better to give birth in hospital?' I asked.

Sadaatu said that in some ways she preferred the traditional way of being seated to give birth but in hospital she had to lie on a bed. She explained that some women were afraid of going to hospital because evil spirits could put a spell on the afterbirth but now hospitals allow mothers to bring the afterbirth home so they can bury it in their compound away from harmful spirits.

When I asked about post-natal care Sadaatu said that mothers receive help from relatives for three months after the birth of the first child but less for subsequent children. It is the custom to give the mother meals of meat from a cow's leg or chicken for the first seven days or longer depending on the family circumstances. Glancing at her husband she said that in many cases husbands help their wives by bringing water and firewood until they are strong again. She finished by saying that all women were encouraged to take their children for inoculations but this was only really possible for those living in Mubi.

There was the sound of scuffling feet outside and two faces peered in the doorway. Hajara started to tell her brothers to leave us but, not wishing to outstay my welcome, I thanked her parents for inviting me to their home. I could see that Sadaatu was becoming tired with the effort of answering my questions and I thanked her again.

On the short drive back Hajara told me that her mother had married into a blacksmith family and her paternal grandmother had been a witch doctor although her parents had been Muslim for as long as she could remember. Unfortunately we reached the secondary school before I had the opportunity to pursue the subject. However it gave me a glimpse of how traditional and modern beliefs were interconnected.

The girls had obviously enjoyed their time away from school and we made arrangements to see Hannatu's family the following week.

# Chapter 10　Hannatu's mother delivers a baby

Hannatu's family lived in Njaira which was on the main road a couple of miles west of Mubi and mainly consisted of round huts with thatched roofs. I parked the car just off the road and Hajara and I followed Hannatu to her parents' compound. Apart from a few chickens scratching in the dust there was no one about although we could hear wailing in the distance.

'I think someone has died,' said Hannatu.

'Perhaps we should come back another day,' I said trying to keep the disappointment from my voice.

'No, it will be fine. Come!'

As Hannatu led the way the wailing became louder and I felt shivers down my spine. We came to a mud walled compound with people spilling out of the entrance.

'Wait here,' said Hannatu and made her way towards the lamenting, swaying people. Most of the women wore brightly coloured wrappers and head scarves but a few were clad in aprons of leaves around their waist.

'This is a Pagan village,' whispered Hajara. 'But Hannatu's family are Christian,' she added when I looked surprised.

I watched as Hannatu spoke rapidly to an elderly woman and gesticulated in my direction. The woman nodded and slipped into the compound. A few minutes later a couple in their fifties emerged and walked slowly towards us, stopping every now and again to greet people. Hannatu introduced her father, Jacob, and her mother, Mary, and explained that I had come to find out about pregnancy and childbirth customs.

'Maybe this isn't a good time,' I said but Jacob nodded encouragingly and Hannatu explained that her parents had paid their respects to the deceased and would return the next day for the funeral.

We walked back to the compound and Jacob brought a

folding wooden chair for me to sit on while he, Mary and the girls made themselves comfortable on grass mats. Unlike Sadaatu's husband, he was interested in the conversation and asked me questions about how things were in my country. I only gave brief answers because, as I sat in their compound, the gulf between our experiences seemed too great. I knew that Hannatu had four brothers but was shocked when Mary told me that she had given birth to ten children but only five had lived. I murmured my sympathy but didn't like to pursue the subject especially as they were obviously proud of their surviving children.

When I asked if the wife tells her husband as soon as she knows she is pregnant Mary looked at Jacob and laughed, saying that it is not the custom but he can usually tell. She added that some women tell a sister-in-law or a friend who pass on the news to the husband. They told me about various taboos but it wasn't clear if they believed in them. One example they gave was that pregnant women are forbidden to walk after dark as there is a night bird that can cause the baby to die. Similarly, pregnant women must keep away from trees near water as the spirits that live there may kill the baby.

Mary said that she had only been to the ante-natal clinic in Mubi once because they had pressed her stomach so hard that she was in pain for a week and she was afraid to go again. Hannatu told me that her mother is the only 'old woman' in the village who helps at childbirths and she had been doing this for the last ten years because she liked to help people. Jacob nodded approvingly and added that she only went if she was asked and that sometimes she was paid but often people simply gave their thanks.

'How is Ester?' asked Hannatu. Turning to me she added, 'We were at primary school together but she only stayed three years'.

'Ester is well. She will deliver soon.'

'Will she go to hospital?' asked Hajara.

Mary shook her head. 'She says she would rather

deliver at home.'

'But it's her first baby! And Mubi is near.' Hannatu looked disapproving.

'If there is trouble she will go,' her mother said calmly.

There was silence and I guessed the girls were thinking the same as me that, with no telephones or ambulance service, getting to hospital quickly could be difficult.

'Is she at home now? Perhaps we can ask her some questions,' I suggested eagerly.

Jacob looked at his wife. 'Let us take our friend to meet the Chief first.'

I blushed, worried that I had been pushy. What right did I have to wander round their village with my questions?

Jacob smiled at me as he spoke to his daughter.

'My father says that what you are doing is good but some people may not understand so it is best that we meet our Chief first.'

Shadows were beginning to lengthen and as it cooled down the village had come alive. Children were playing, women were pounding corn for the evening meal and every now and again we paused to greet people coming from the compound of the deceased person.

'There he is,' said Hannatu as we reached a well where children jostled with each other as they waited their turn to draw water. Sitting cross-legged under a silk cotton tree was an elderly man wearing a short white robe and turban. He was holding a small wooden spindle and concentrating on the thread he was spinning from cotton fibre. I watched, fascinated as more and more thread emerged.

'This is our Chief' said Jacob and introduced me.

I wasn't quite sure how to react as the Chief continued spinning but he listened intently as Jacob explained who I was and what I was doing in Njairi. When he reached a point where he felt he could stop spinning, the Chief stood up and welcomed me to the village. He said something to Hannatu which obviously pleased her.

'He's saying that she's a credit to her parents and the

village,' whispered Hajara.

They spoke for a few more minutes then we took our leave.

As we were heading towards my car a woman hurried towards Mary, speaking rapidly and gesticulating to a nearby compound.

'I think Ester's time has come,' whispered Hannatu.

Mary said that she had to go and help but, knowing my interest in childbirth, she invited me to go with her.

'Ester's husband is a soldier in the south so she has returned home to deliver her first child. She is staying in her sister's house,' explained Hannatu.

Children were playing in the compound and a young woman was pounding corn. She put down her pestle and, rubbing the sweat from her forehead, listened intently as Mary explained why we had come. She nodded and indicated that we could go inside.

It was dark in the hut and Ester had her back to the door. She was sitting bolt upright on a low stool absolutely motionless and had apparently been in labour all day. An old woman was sitting in the shadows at the back of the hut and there was a rapid exchange as Mary questioned them.

'The woman is Ester's grandmother,' Hannatu told me in a low voice.'

I was aware that it was getting late.

'I think we should go now.' I said, feeling out of place as the three of us hovered behind the silent young woman.

When Hannatu passed on my thanks to her mother she said I should return the following day to see the baby.

My mind was racing as I drove back, taking care to avoid people strolling in the middle of the road and slamming on the brakes as a motor cycle overtaking a lorry barely missed us.

'Will you return tomorrow?' asked Hannatu.

'Are you free?'

'No, we have an extra class tomorrow. But you can go.'

The sun was hot and there was no shade when I parked near Mary and Jacob's compound.

'Koko!' I said, clapping my hands at the entrance but no one was at home so, feeling slightly apprehensive, I made my way to Ester's sister's compound.

A girl about ten years old was sitting outside.

'Mary inside?' I enquired after greeting her in Hausa.

She frowned then nodded as she recognised me and beckoned me to follow her.

Ester was no longer sitting on the birthing stool but lying on a low raffia bed and Mary was sitting on the floor next to her. Without the students to interpret I felt ill at ease and dreadfully sorry for the girl who was now in her second day of labour. Clumsily I searched in my bag and handed Mary a bottle of water.

'For Ester', I said awkwardly.

Mary nodded, opened the bottle and tilted Ester's head who took a sip of water.

The old woman I had seen the previous day muttered something but her face was in shadow so I could not guess what she was saying.

A look of irritation crossed Mary's face and she turned to me and shook her head as she said quietly that Ester should go to hospital.

'Perhaps I could take her in the car,' I said.

Mary shrugged and, gesturing towards me, spoke to the woman in the shadows who appeared to vehemently reject my suggestion.

I leant against the wall of the hut, unnerved by the air of resignation and my own impotence. Although, like most mothers, I had experienced regular periods of boredom since Melinda was born I wasn't adjusted to the African way of being able to sit and wait for whatever was going to happen.

It wasn't long before I found the fetid atmosphere claustrophobic and, with a nod in Mary's direction, I began to back out of the door.

'Sai Gobe', I said wondering if I really meant that I

would return tomorrow.

In fact I did return the following day at lunch time, the quietest time of the day. The door to the compound was locked and no one was about. I made my way to Mary and Jacob's compound but no one was there either. As I drove back I wondered whether to stop at the hospital to check if Ester was there but instead I hurried home to Melinda and Adrian.

*** 

A few days later I picked up Hannatu and Hajara and we set off for Njairi. As we approached the compound we could hear the sound of chopping wood. Mary wasn't in but Jacob put down his axe and told us that Ester was at home having delivered her baby in hospital.

'That's wonderful news!' I said. Then as an afterthought asked, 'Is the baby well?'

'My father says we should visit her.'

Not knowing what we would find I followed Hannatu as she led the way.

Ester was sitting near the door of the hut breast-feeding a tiny baby. She looked tired but smiled when she saw us. Hannatu tried to ask about the birth but Ester was immersed in feeding her baby who was sucking well. I asked if I could take a photo but it was too dark and my flash didn't work. I could see that the woman sitting at the back of the hut was becoming agitated by our presence so I gave the child a one naira note and suggested we leave.

When we were out of earshot Hajara exclaimed that she had never seen such a tiny baby. Hannatu agreed although her mother had told her about delivering premature babies who had lived. She explained that, as long as the mother rested for two to three months and was given good food to eat so that her milk would flow the baby would be fine.

'I don't understand Ester's reluctance to go to hospital in good time,' I said.

'I think she wanted to,' replied Hannatu, 'but her

grandmother was worried about the afterbirth. Anyway, it's safely buried in the compound.'

Hajara looked sceptical. 'How do you know that?'

'I noticed the earth had been freshly dug near the washing hut.' Hannatu explained that the afterbirth was often buried near the place where the mother took her bath.

We heard music and passed a crowd of children watching an older boy strumming on a small wooden instrument.

'Will there be music at the naming ceremony?' I asked.

'Yes, there will be a big celebration as the child is boy. It will take place when the father has leave to return from the South.

We called in to say goodbye to Jacob who was still chopping wood then I drove the girls back to the secondary school in time for supper.

# Chapter 11    Two families in Lamurde

We met Jim and Nancy Hoskinson and their children when we were visiting our friends at Kulp Bible School. I was intrigued when they told me they were translating the Bible into Gude and even more so when they said they lived in Lamurde. They were interested when I told them about my research and invited me to visit any time except market day. They said they lived near the church and I would recognise their car parked outside their compound.

The following week Melinda and I were bumping along the rutted track into Lamurde village. We drove across a low wooden bridge over a stream and past the church. I saw Jim's car parked nearby and we came to a halt outside a large compound surrounded by a low fence.

The gate was open and Melinda ran ahead when we heard children's voices. I hurried after her past several huts then stopped in confusion when I saw an elderly woman sitting on the ground shelling groundnuts and looking at Melinda in surprise.

'I'm sorry, I thought this was Nancy's compound.'

'Nancy lives that way.' The woman pointed to a large rectangular hut at the other end of the compound.

'Thank you.' I felt puzzled as I took Melinda's hand and walked past a washing area and latrine.

'So you came. Welcome!' Jim, dressed in shorts and a check shirt, hurried out of the building followed by two little girls. They eyed Melinda suspiciously for a moment then the eldest, who was about five years old, held out her hand and led Melinda round the building.

'Nancy's out back with the baby. She'll be pleased to see you.'

I followed Jim past a bed of marigolds which gave a patch of colour to the compacted earth of the small area where Melinda and the other children were already absorbed in building a tower of wooden blocks.

'So you found us,' Nancy said in a soft American

85

accent as she jiggled her youngest daughter on her knee.

'Yes, although I wasn't sure if I had the right place,' I replied as Jim brought two more chairs.

'You were surprised it doesn't look like an ex-pat's house,' Jim laughed.

I smiled, not quite knowing what to say.

'We rent this half of the compound from Mr Musa; you met his wife as you came in.'

'Our organisation prefers that we live among the people whose language we are translating,' said Nancy.

'How's the translating going?' I asked politely.

'Well, thank you,' said Jim, 'but it can be slow sometimes.'

'I suppose it can be difficult in the evenings.' I glanced at the dark interior of their living space.

'We have oil lamps and I like to start work at first light.'

'You told us last week that you're looking for women to talk to about childbirth customs.' Nancy stood up and sat the baby on the ground with the other children.

'Yes. The Gude students who are helping me in Lamurde are boys and there are some questions I don't feel comfortable asking them to interpret.'

'I would like to help you. I know someone we can visit now if you like.'

'Who are you thinking of visiting?' A look of alarm flickered across Jim's face as the tower the children were building came tumbling down.

'Mariama. We won't be long. The girls will be fine. You can give them some orange cordial. You don't mind leaving Melinda for a little while?' Nancy asked me as an afterthought.

'No, if that's all right with you, Jim.' I had brought my notebook with me but had really intended this to be a social visit.

'It's just fine.' But by the puzzled look on Jim's face I guessed that Nancy was acting out of character.

'Usually the women are working on their farms at this time,' said Nancy as we walked past the church to a compound with a battered pick-up truck parked outside. 'But the family are building a new hut for their eldest son and his bride so Mariama is at home cooking for the men.'

'Do you know how many children they have?'

'Five, I think. They are a Christian family,' she added.

We could hear male voices and the sounds of hammering as we approached.

Nancy clapped her hands at the gate and Mariama's husband hurried towards us frowning slightly. However, he greeted us cordially and led us to the small kitchen area where his wife was standing at a table washing some decorated spoons made from calabashes.

She lowered her eyes when Nancy explained the purpose of our visit. I asked if this was a convenient time for her but, as far as I could tell, Nancy did not translate this. Instead she asked me to give her the list of questions I had prepared. As Nancy read, then slowly translated the questions, I wished that we had had the opportunity to go over them first.

'Who do you first tell when you are pregnant?' asked Nancy in a business like voice.

Mariama put her hand on her stomach before answering in a monotone.

Nancy listened carefully then said, 'She might tell a close sister-in-law but prefers to wait as long as possible because she doesn't want people to know in case she has the shame of having a girl.'

I didn't ask whether she had boys or girls and wondered what she thought of Nancy's three daughters.

Mariama resumed her spoon washing while Nancy asked the next question.

'She says that she did not do anything special when she was pregnant although she went to the ante-natal clinic in Mubi.'

The question: 'Should you eat any special food in pregnancy?' made Mariama think carefully before saying that if the baby the mother is carrying refuses to eat meat or fish then the mother can't eat it.

She told us that most pregnant women work until the birth of their baby then shook her head vigorously when Nancy asked about taboos, saying that she didn't know of any.

Nancy was about to ask another question when we heard the distant ringing of the school bell announcing the mid-morning break. I could see that Mariama was uncomfortable and I thought longingly of the cordial Nancy had promised the children.

'I think we should go,' I said. 'Please thank Mariama for telling me about her customs.'

As we walked back past the church Nancy introduced me to the Pastor who had just got off his bicycle. He welcomed me to the village and suggested I talk to his wife sometime.

Jim looked relieved to see us when we returned to find the girls busy drawing. I was glad they were using coloured pencils as Melinda was going through a stage of eating any wax crayons I gave her.

Over a cup of orange cordial we told Jim about our visit to Mariama and about the Pastor's suggestion that I should talk to his wife.

However, although I visited Lamurde a couple of weeks later, it wasn't until after Christmas that Nancy and I visited the Pastor's wife. She had recently given birth to her seventh child, a daughter, in Mubi hospital. Her eldest daughter had just finished primary school and was eager to act as our interpreter. The Pastor listened to our conversation from his room and occasionally expanded on his daughter's translation. Mother and baby were well and I left with a feeling of satisfaction.

# Chapter 12    Awo and the sacred cave

Melinda had a cough so I decided not to take her on my next visit to Lamurde with Marcus and Ahmed. It was a Sunday morning and people dressed in their best clothes were spilling out of the church as I drove through the village towards Lamurde Mountain. Although the rainy season was drawing to a close the hills were still green with a scattering of trees in full leaf. Interspersed among the compounds were clumps of groundnuts and rows of guinea corn ready to harvest.

I parked under the shade of a mango tree and followed the students up the rough track to Lamurde Wamngo. The witchdoctor's compound was hidden behind a euphorbia hedge growing between large boulders. We stopped at a roughly made wooden door and Ahmed clapped his hands to indicate our presence. A man in his twenties greeted us enthusiastically as he recognised Ahmed. He didn't seem surprised to see me and I realised that my previous visit would not have gone unnoticed in this small community.

Awo was sitting on the floor making a small wooden birthing stool. He acknowledged us but made no attempt to stop what he was doing although he seemed happy enough to answer my questions. One of the women I had seen previously brought me a woven mat to sit on. She then sat down on the bare earth with her legs stretched out in front of her and a calabash of groundnuts which she began to shell.

Several children appeared from behind the hut. 'Good morning. How are you?' asked the biggest boy gravely.

When I replied his sisters giggled behind their hands and Ahmed spoke sharply to them. A couple more women appeared and settled down to listen.

Although he did not look up from his carving, the witchdoctor took each of my questions seriously. He told me that if a woman comes to him for protection during her pregnancy he gives her a charm made from twine and feathers from a dove to tie round her waist to keep away evil spirits. I realised that I had noticed something similar on several of the young women from the hills who passed by our house on their way to market.

Awo said that he was able to cure morning sickness by giving special medicine from the bush. He was also able give medicine to make the afterbirth come.

I asked if the witch doctor was called during the birth and he said only if there is a problem. If labour is prolonged he would tie a charm around the mother's neck similar to that round the waist but with white paper and animal skin instead of dove feathers.

However, when I asked about breach births he stopped his carving, shook his head and spoke rapidly. I sensed a feeling of agitation amongst the women.

'Awo lost a child that way,' said Marcus quietly. 'He says that things are better now we have the hospital in Mubi but it is important that the mother gets there in time if the baby is in the wrong position.'

Having just walked up the rocky path to Lamurde Wamngo I couldn't imagine how it would be possible for a woman in that condition to get out of the village, let alone to the hospital without adequate transport. I had often seen women riding on bicycle cross bars but that would have been an uncomfortable and dangerous option under those circumstances.

'Please tell Awo I am sorry for his loss,' I said inadequately.

I was wondering whether we should take our leave when the man who had let us in spoke to Ahmed.

'He says that Awo is famous for his powers of divination,' said Ahmed.

I felt a frisson of excitement but turned my mind to the subject in hand and asked if he was able to tell the sex of a child before birth.

Awo gesticulated as he began to explain how he carried out a divination.

He got up and placed a clay pot filled with sand in front

of him and invited me to look at the objects inside. On one side were pieces of string, broken shells, seeds, groundnuts and a few coins. In the centre was half a calabash stuck in the sand. On the other side were six large snail shells. Awo squatted in front of the pot and placed some seeds near the shells.

Marcus edged closer as he translated. 'The seeds represent male and female'.

We watched as Awo put three sticks in the sand by the rim of the pot.

'The largest stick is the god stick and the others are male and female,' said Marcus.

Speaking softly, the witchdoctor trailed the god stick over the sand then pulled the half calabash so that the snails and seeds were pushed towards the male and female sticks. When he stopped pushing, he stared intently at the new position of the seeds.

'Your next child will be a boy,' he pronounced solemnly.

Everyone looked pleased.

Awo swept the sand with his hand and replaced the snails and sticks.

'He wants to know if there is anything you want. He will do another divination if you give him fifty kobo,' said Ahmed.

I thought for a moment. 'I want to know if my daughter's cough will get better soon,' I said as I handed over the coin.

Awo put the coin with the others then added two more sticks around the rim of the pot and pointed to each one.

'God stick, your daughter, you, your husband, the cough,' translated Ahmed.

Once again the witchdoctor trailed the god stick over the sand then pulled the half calabash so the snails were pushed towards the sticks.

This divination took longer and we waited with bated breath for the diagnosis.

'Your daughter's cough will get better sooner or later.'

91

The sincerity in his voice was unmistakeable and I felt a sense of relief as I watched him discard the cough stick, replace the shells and pull the calabash again.

The students nodded in agreement as Awo said that my husband is always with my daughter and loves her very much. Then there was a burst of laughter when he continued that my husband loves me so much that he cannot describe it. Finally he announced that I was not yet pregnant but wanted to have many children.

This seemed an appropriate time to take our leave so I stood up and asked the students to relay my thanks and say how interesting everything had been.

A rapid conversation ensued as the witchdoctor pointed downhill to a part of the village I hadn't visited.

'He would like to show you his sacred cave,' said Marcus in an awed voice. 'We must come in the morning on a market day and he will explain everything to us.'

'That would be an honour,' I replied.

I arranged to pick up Marcus on the first Wednesday of the holidays. As Awo had predicted, Melinda had recovered from her cough but we thought it would not be appropriate to take her on this occasion.

***

Marcus was waiting for me outside his parents' compound. As I got out of the car I noticed that he looked older without his school uniform. I was wearing a long java print skirt with matching top and headscarf which was comfortable and relatively cool.

It was with some trepidation that I followed Marcus along a narrow path with vegetation growing high on either side. Despite the shade, I was sweating as we trudged up a side of Lamurde Mountain that was unfamiliar to me. Occasionally I heard muffled voices drifting from the village. A movement in the bushes stopped us both in our tracks and I could see that Marcus

92

was as shaken as I was when a snake glided in front of us and into the undergrowth. We waited for a moment and then continued until we heard the trickling of a stream.

'We are nearly there,' whispered Marcus pointing to some pieces of pottery on the side of the path.

Ahead of us was a canopy of trees across a stream.

'We go this way.'

The path had petered out and I followed Marcus, stepping in between rocks and tufts of vegetation beside the stream until we came to a clearing. In front of us was a rock outcrop forming a natural cave. A tangle of creeping plants hung down from the roof. Seated on a rock at the entrance to the cave was the witchdoctor. He was dressed in a faded brown caftan and embroidered hat.

Marcus bowed his head and greeted him in Gude then squatted on his haunches in front of him. He translated Awo's words of welcome to me and indicated that I should sit on a low boulder. I murmured my thanks which Marcus translated at length.

For a moment I felt suspended in time. I knew there was no urgency but in my western way I hurried to fill the silence. I pointed to the upturned clay pots and calabashes strewn haphazardly at the back of the cave and asked who had brought them and why they visited the shrine.

Awo spoke at some length. After a while Marcus explained that people brought offerings in pots or calabashes and left them for the god Lara who was one of the smaller gods of the clan. He said that women would visit the shrine if they had something particular they wanted to ask the god. Their questions often centred around wanting to conceive a child and keep healthy during pregnancy.

I had been looking intently at the collection of pottery when I noticed a fresh corn cob at the front of the cave.

'Is that an offering?' I asked, frustrated that I couldn't speak the language.

'People often visit the shrine on their way to market and leave a small gift. On their return they leave something they have bought like a small cake.'

We heard voices and two young women appeared from the other side of the stream. They looked surprised to see me and spoke laughingly to Marcus. He shifted uncomfortably and I guessed they were making a joke about him being in the company of a young white woman. I smiled at them from my boulder that was becoming increasingly uncomfortable. The women each laid a cola nut near the corn cob and departed on their way.

Awo had an amused expression as he spoke to Marcus.

I guessed that Marcus only translated part of what was said. 'Is there anything else you would like to know?' he asked.

I knew I would have lots more questions later but my mind was befuddled with the heat and the strangeness of the situation. I stood up and thanked Awo for inviting me to his sacred cave. Then, rather diffidently, I asked if I could take some photographs.

Awo stood aside and gestured to the cave. My hand was shaking as I looked through the view finder of my little instamatic camera. Then, with a click, an image of Awo's sacred cave was recorded.

# Chapter 13    Christmas in Mubi

I was deep in thought as I followed Marcus back to my car parked outside his parents' compound.

'Perhaps I should greet your parents,' I said, not wanting to break the spell and return to reality.

Marcus shook his head. 'They will be at market.' He hesitated. 'Please, Madam, can you give me a lift, I would like to visit a friend in Mubi.'

'Of course,' I answered, pleased to have his company on the drive back. 'Where shall I drop you?'

'The town centre, near the market.'

We passed several lorries laden with passengers and goods heading into Mubi.

I drove slowly down the dirt road leading to the market past a group of children playing tag and stopped outside the bank.

'Let me get you a cold drink,' I said.

We went into the only shop in the area with a refrigerator and I bought us both a bottle of Sprite. Marcus thanked me and asked politely if I was going to the market.

'I had better get back,' I said.

We walked towards the market and paused when we reached the car.

'I am sorry my parents were not in today,' said Marcus. 'They say you are welcome to visit any time.'

'That would be nice; perhaps we will come after Christmas.'

'Till the next time.' Marcus smiled and began to walk away.

'Hello, Heather,' said a familiar voice.

'Hello,' I replied in confusion as the Principal came out of the bank with his wife. She looked cool in a pretty floral dress and I suddenly felt awkward in my Nigerian style skirt and head scarf.

I fiddled with my empty Sprite bottle. 'Isn't it hot

today,' I said.

'It's cooler than Maiduguri, we're pleased to be back,' said the Principal's wife.

'It's still hot though,' I gabbled. 'It was really hot at the sacred cave.'

There was a stunned silence and I felt mortified.

'You didn't go there on your own?' The Principal looked concerned.

'No I went with Marcus. Awo invited us.'

'Marcus is an excellent student.' He paused then continued quietly, 'The District Commissioner was asking me about you a few days ago. He said the authorities know about your work and he thinks what you are doing is a good thing as long as you never go into the villages alone.'

I was taken aback. 'How does he know?'

'It's his business to know what goes on. He told me that Mubi is proud of its reputation of welcoming people of all religions and it's important for everyone to tolerate each other.'

'Oh, yes, that's what I think.' The niggling worry I had felt since starting my research began to lift.

He smiled, 'So carry on the good work.'

'I will. Thank you.' I scrabbled for my keys and unlocked the car.

*** 

There was a white Peugot 204 parked outside our house when I arrived home. For a moment I was irritated, thinking I wasn't in the mood for guests. Then I realised it was Jill and Dave's car. When we had last seen them in Maiduguri they told us they planned to spend Christmas on the Mambilla Plateau and we had invited them to break their journey with us on their way south.

Melinda toddled round the corner of the house shouting 'Mima!'

'Are Jill and Dave here? That's lovely!' I said as I kissed my daughter.

She took my hand and pulled me to the veranda where Jemima was playing with Melinda's toys and Adrian, Jill and Dave were drinking iced tea.

'It's lovely to see you. You'll stay the night, won't you?' I paused and looked at Jill. 'Where's your sister? I thought you planned to take her with you to Mambilla.'

Jill's face crumpled. 'She's been deported!'

'Oh my God!' I sat down. 'What happened?'

'She didn't have the right visa,' said Dave. 'The authorities agreed Josie could have a ten month visa to stay and look after Jemima until we went home at the end of my contract but there was a muddle and she ended up with a tourist visa. An immigration official called at the house and demanded her passport. He said she was being deported the next day because she was taking a job that could be done by a Nigerian.'

'We were both teaching,' continued Jill. 'Poor Josie, she was in a real state when we got home.'

'How awful! What did you do?'

'We rushed round packing her things and Dave drove her to Kano very early the next morning.'

Dave frowned as he took up the story. 'She's only seventeen. When we got to the airport we found the plane was full of people going to England for Christmas. An immigration official told the airline to bump off two passengers so that Josie and another deportee could get on the flight. She was escorted on to the plane and then given back her passport.'

'Poor Josie. She must have been very upset.'

'We all are. Jemima keeps looking for her.' Jill bit her lip.

'What will you do?' I asked sympathetically although I guessed the answer.

'I've resigned from my job. What else could I do?'

I couldn't think of anything to say and the four of us sat in silence watching the girls playing.

Ahmadu appeared from the servants' quarter. 'Shall I prepare lunch Madam?'

I got up. 'Yes, I'll help you'

Over lunch we talked about their planned trip.

'We were going to take Josie to Mambilla while she was here so we thought we would go ahead anyway,' said Jill as she spooned food into Jemima's mouth.

'It's supposed to be beautiful and a lot cooler. But it's an awful long way.' I deftly moved my glass of filtered water from Melinda's reach.

Jemima spluttered and spat out her food which Jill calmly mopped up.

'We had planned the trip knowing that Josie would be with us. Dave and I were going to share the driving while Josie looked after Jemima.'

'Where are you thinking of staying?'

'There are rest houses along the way and we've got the names of some British VSO teachers at the school in Gembu.'

I knew it was the custom for ex-pats to offer hospitality. We had given and been the recipients of hospitality, both in Nigeria and when travelling in Ghana.

Jemima began to cough.

'I think it's time for her medicine. Did we bring the cool bag from the car?'

Adrian got up. 'Dave gave me the medicine to put in the fridge. You mustn't forget it in the morning.' He glanced at me and raised his eyebrows.

'You're welcome to stay longer,' I said in response to Adrian's unspoken suggestion. 'You can spend Christmas with us if you like.'

Jill hesitated. 'That's very kind. But we'll be all right, won't we Dave?'

He nodded. 'Oh yes, we'll be all right.'

The following morning we tried to persuade our friends to stay but they were determined to keep to their plan.

'You know you're welcome if it doesn't work out,' I said as we helped them load their car.

'Thank you.' A look of relief flashed across Dave's face. 'We might just take you up on the offer.'

'Whatever you decide, you must stop on your return and tell us what it's like,' I said.

'We will! And thanks for having us.'

'Bye Mima!' shouted Melinda as we watched them drive away.

*\*\*\**

'I'm going across to the staff room to check my pigeon hole for mail; do you want to come?' asked Adrian.

'No, I'll tidy up here but you can take Melinda.'

I went into the kitchen where a large pot of water was bubbling on the cooker. I switched off the gas, took a jar of allum from the top shelf and put a pinch of the white powder into the pot to settle the clay granules. When all the particles had sunk to the bottom Ahmadu would pour the water into a gallon size filter next to the fridge.

I checked the freezer compartment and was thankful that Adrian had removed the snake he had kept there for several weeks waiting for the appropriate point in the science curriculum to use as a visual aid. Needless to say, it was a very successful lesson.

As I wandered into the front garden I could see Adrian and Melinda talking to Victoria who was sitting in her usual position outside Richard's house. I still felt bad about her peremptory dismissal although she appeared to bear us no ill will.

Adrian waved and arrived just as Clive's car turned into our drive.

'Hello! Where's Adelchi?' I asked as Clive and the children got out.

'She's packing. I wonder if you could look after the kids for a couple of hours?'

'Yes, of course. Is everything all right?'

Clive looked flustered. 'I'm being transferred to Gembu Secondary School on the Mambilla Plateau. They want me to take over as Principal.'

'Congratulations!' Adrian and I said in unison.

99

'The current principal has left and they need someone to take over immediately,' Clive said with a mixture of pride and apprehension.

'When do you leave? Will you be here for Christmas?'

Clive shook his head. 'We'll spend Christmas with Adelchi's parents in Numan and continue to Gembu.'

'How far is it from there?' asked Adrian.

'About three hundred miles.'

'That's doable in a day.'

'Clive looked doubtful. 'Once you get to the bottom of the plateau the road is really bad. But we'll manage. You must come and visit us when we've settled in.'

I told Clive about Jill and Dave on their way to Mambilla but when I mentioned Jemima he frowned.

'I don't think I would take a nine month old baby on that journey if I didn't have to. Do they know people there?'

I thought it best not to mention that they hoped to stay at the secondary school in Gembu. 'We've said they can spend Christmas with us if they change their mind,' I said instead.

'Can we do anything to help with packing?' asked Adrian.

'Not at the moment but it would be great if you can look after the children for a couple of hours.'

I glanced at Helen and Philip who were already playing with Melinda. 'You'll need longer than that. We'll bring them back this afternoon.'

'Thank you; that would be a real help. Bye kids, be good for Heather and Adrian.'

'Bye Dad!' they called, scarcely looking up from their game.

'It's great about Clive's promotion but awful to have no say in the matter. What if you were suddenly transferred?' I said as Clive drove away.

'Oh we'd cope,' Adrian said cheerfully. 'But it's not likely to happen as my contract finishes in six months.'

As we predicted, Jill and Dave returned a couple of days later. The constant dust from the laterite roads had made Jemima's cough worse.

'We were following a grader on a stretch of road where it was impossible to overtake and it threw up so much dust it was difficult to see.' Jill pushed her hand through her hair which had gone several shades lighter due to the dust.

'We'll heat some water for the girls' bath later. The hot water heater was never fitted so we can only offer you a cold shower, but the water pressure is good at the moment,' I said as we helped them unpack the car.

'You've come in time to help us get a Christmas tree,' said Adrian. 'We had planned to go into the bush tomorrow to see if we could find something suitable.

The following day Jemima's cough had cleared so we all piled into our car and drove slowly along the bush road at the back of our house to Digil, a village near a small river that flowed throughout the year.

Two women had just finished their washing. One was putting clothes on the rocks to dry next to an empty packet of Omo washing powder and the other woman was issuing instructions to a couple of boys who were fishing. She turned and stared at us. Melinda ran up to her and Jemima, who Jill was carrying, held out her arms. Jill automatically passed her to the woman who chuckled in delight and called to her friend who hurried over to see the 'baturi' children.

It felt good to be chatting in sign language without an interpreter. This was simple interaction about our children and the fish the women hoped their sons would bring home for the evening meal. They let out a peal of laughter and wagged their fingers in disbelief when Adrian indicated that when he was a boy he had caught a very large fish. Then the woman holding Jemima handed her back to Jill and they went on their way.

Adrian returned to the car and picked up the machete

and the cold box while Dave put Jemima in her sling. Jill and I brought the water cooler and a blanket. We walked along a narrow path beside the river until we came to a tree giving plenty of shade.

Melinda wanted to paddle but, although the fast flowing water was probably safe from bilharzia, we decided not to risk it.

'Our students often have to go to the hospital for a course of injections for bilharzia they catch when they walk through shallow water,' said Adrian as he spread out the blanket for us to sit on.

After our picnic Adrian and Dave selected a branch from a bush with small dark leaves which seemed suitable for a Christmas tree. They cut it down and dragged it to where we were sitting.

'Perhaps we should be getting back', I said seeing Jill yawn. 'I expect you're still tired after the long journey.

As we retraced our steps we saw two men wading in the river. They were wearing red swimming trunks and each was holding a wooden sieve which they skimmed just below the surface of the water. After a few minutes one of the men waded into the centre of the river and emptied his sieve into a metal dish balanced on a rock.

'They're panning for something.' Adrian looked intently. 'It must be gravel. I'll see more with my telephoto lens.' He pointed his camera and took several pictures.

The men were so intent on what they were doing that they did not look up until they were disturbed by Melinda's chatter. The man nearest the bank waved then continued sieving gravel from the clay.

I thought of the heavy machinery involved in the gravel pits near where I grew up in Surrey and looked again at the men bent double in the fast flowing water that came half way to their knees.

'What a hard way to earn a living,' I said, blinking as I felt sweat running down my face and was relieved when we reached the car.

***

'Are you sure you want us to stay for Christmas?' Jill asked the next morning.

'Of course! It'll be lovely doing Christmas together.'

I looked at Melinda showing Jemima how to build a tower with her building blocks.

'Shall we pop into town? Can you keep an eye on the girls?' I asked Adrian and Dave who were comparing notes on science teaching.

Fifteen minutes later I parked outside the bookshop.

'Oh! You've got an SPCK!' said Jill.

We looked in the window at the display of Bibles, Hausa dictionaries and a colourful book of West African birds.

'Do you buy many books from here?' asked Jill.

'A few. They sometimes have nice children's books.'

I was about to ask Jill if she wanted to browse round the shop when I was greeted by Maliki, the art teacher. I introduced him to Jill and said that she was visiting from Maiduguri.

'That is my home town,' he said as he shook her hand. 'I'm going there today. I wish you a very happy Christmas.'

I knew that Maliki was a Muslim and I was touched. 'Thank you. And I wish you a very good New Year,' I replied.

'What a good looking man!' exclaimed Jill when Maliki was out of earshot.

'He is, isn't he? All the girls are in love with him.'

We made our way into the market and stopped at a stall selling beautifully decorated calabashes. Jill bought two small ones and we wandered further into the market.

Several tailors were sitting over their treadle sewing machines.

'This is where Helen and I come to have our clothes made,' I said. 'People appreciate us wearing locally made clothes and the tailors can copy anything.'

103

I introduced Jill to the tailor who had recently made me a long skirt and matching blouse. He tried to persuade her to let him make something for her and she said she would when she had found some cloth she liked.

We walked further into the market where a group of women were selling pots.

'Oh look! There's Marcus's mother.'

I greeted her in Hausa then stopped, feeling at a loss without Marcus to translate.

'What beautiful pots!' said Jill and pointed to some tall water containers burnished the colour of red ochre.

Marcus's mother smiled and, turning to the other women, explained who I was. Then, with promises to meet again soon, we went on our way.

We wandered around, pausing to buy mangoes and guavas, then headed back to the car.

'It's a lovely market,' said Jill, 'lots going on but not huge like Maiduguri.'

'It's about the only thing to see in Mubi! I hope you won't be bored spending Christmas with us.

'Your garden's nicer than ours, hardly anything grows where we live. And I loved our walk yesterday. It's lovely to get out into the hills.'

'We can do that again. And we'll have a Boxing Day party and invite our friends with children.'

We all got on so well that Jill, Dave and Jemima stayed till New Year's Day. On their last evening we sat under the stars and talked about our plans for the future.

When we were on leave the previous summer Adrian had been offered a science teaching job in Lincolnshire starting in September 1976.

'That was lucky. Will you stay there for long?' asked Dave.

'I doubt it, we'd like to put down some roots in England but then look for another teaching contract in Africa. What are your plans?'

'We don't really mind where we live, it depends on the job.'

'It's nice that we're going back at the same time,' said Jill, 'we can keep in touch.

I raised my glass. 'To the future.'

'And our friendship,' added Jill as we clinked glasses.

# Chapter 14  What happened in Gwoza

We were pleased to see Kitty, Dick and Melissa when they returned from their leave in the USA. We suggested that we took a trip to Boukoula, the border post with Cameroon, just past Sahuda. So, on the last day of the Christmas holiday, I packed a picnic and we set off.

From Dick's station wagon we were able to get a good view of the Yedseram meandering down from the hills. Dick drove slowly, pausing every now and again to greet men carrying dried thatching grass on their heads. Several of the compounds we passed had new roofs which shone like gold in contrast to the older thatch.

'This is a good time of the year,' said Dick. 'The harvest is in, people have enough to eat and they have time to repair their houses.'

As we passed Sahuda we told them about Pastor Johanna's dam and mentioned that he had learned improved methods of farming when he was a student at Kulp Bible School.

'Perhaps we can call and see them on our way back,' suggested Adrian.

'That would be nice; it's always interesting to see what past students are doing,' said Kitty.'

Dick came to a halt when we reached a concrete post with Boukoula engraved on it. We got out of the station wagon and I took a photograph of everyone smiling at three thousand feet. Below us was the customs post where some men in uniform were standing by a small tin-roofed building. The driver of a lorry parked behind a bar across the road came out of the building, one of the customs officers lifted the bar and the lorry drove from Cameroon into Nigeria.

As the vehicle came slowly up the hill towards us we could see brightly painted slogans including 'Dieu est Amour' on the front. Some of the passengers leant over the side and waved to Melinda and Melissa who waved back.

There was a gust of wind and a ball of dry leaves and grasses skittered towards us. Melinda clapped her hands and began to toddle after it. Melissa took a step forward, unsure whether she was too old to join in now she was four.

'I think it's time for our picnic,' I said.

'What a wonderful view,' said Kitty when we were settled in a patch of shade.

'We love coming here, it's so peaceful,' I agreed.

After lunch the girls ran about collecting fruit pods that had dropped from a nearby baobab tree.

'It feels so soft,' said Melissa stroking the velvety skin.

Two boys carrying sticks appeared and stood watching us. One had a leather bag slung round his shoulder.

'Sannu,' Dick greeted them.

'Kana lahiya,' the eldest replied.

'Lafiya lau,' said Dick. He looked at the boy's bag and, pointing to the baobab pods, asked him in Hausa if they had come to collect the fruit.

The boy replied that they had and pointed to a number of huts in the distance.

Melissa appeared to understand the conversation and began to pass the little collection to the boys who stowed them away in the leather bag. When they had finished the older boy handed back a fruit to the girls. I quickly rummaged in the picnic bag and gave them each an orange each in return.

'Na Gode.' The boys held their hands together as they thanked us.

'Ba kome,' I replied.

We watched for a few minutes as the boys beat the tree with their sticks, causing a few more fruits to fall. Then we packed up our things and drove back to Sahuda.

Apart from a few goats, the village appeared deserted. I led the way past several compounds until we came to Rebecca's home.

'Koko!' I said and clapped my hands at the door in the wall of the compound but there was no reply.

Adrian pointed to the earth dam that Pastor Johanna had built across the river. Two women with baskets on their heads were walking towards us across the dam.

'Maybe they know where the Pastor is,' I said.

As they approached, Kitty asked if they knew where Pastor Johanna and family were. There was a rapid burst of conversation.

'They have gone to a wedding in Mubi', said Kitty. She thanked them and they continued on their way.

'That looks like a very carefully constructed dam,' said Dick. 'Pastor Johanna must be a clever man.'

'Yes, they're a lovely family,' I agreed as we began to retrace our steps to the car.

On the outskirts of Mubi we passed students walking towards the college, some carrying boxes on their heads.

'Are you looking forward to the new term?' asked Dick as he stopped in our drive.

Adrian nodded. 'Quite a lot of this term is taken up with teaching practice which is always interesting.'

'I guess you miss going into schools.' Kitty looked at me sympathetically.

'Yes, but what I'm doing now is just as interesting.'

'Next time you visit us I'll take you to see a Gude family who are in their final year at Kulp.'

'Thank you. Are you coming in for a cup of tea?'

'We should be getting back but it's been lovely spending time with you.'

We arranged to see them in a couple of weeks and waved as they drove off.

***

'I think I'll wander over to college,' said Adrian.

'Okay. Melinda and I will call next door and see if Gail wants to play.

Adrian had only just gone when Hassan appeared with a friend.

'Good afternoon Mrs Rosser. This is Matthew, he is

also a Scout.'

'It's nice to meet you Matthew.' I shook his hand.

'How are you and your daughter?' he asked politely.

'We are well, thank you. Please sit down. I will make us a cool drink.'

I could hear the boys speaking in agitated voices while I was in the kitchen.

'Is everything all right?' I asked as I returned with the drinks.

'No Madam. Something bad has happened.'

I felt a shudder of apprehension as I looked at Hassan's normally cheerful face. 'What?'

'It is Mr Maliki. He is dead.'

I gasped, shocked as I remembered our conversation in Mubi just before Christmas. Malika was a popular teacher and it was difficult to take in what Hassan was saying.

'What happened?'

I was conscious of Matthew staring at the floor and Hassan's fearful expression as he continued.

'There was an accident. In Gwoza. There were three in the car and they hit someone. The two escaped but they killed Mr Maliki.'

'Who did?'

'The Gwoza people.'

'But why?' I stared in disbelief.

'Because they hit a person.'

'Was Mr Maliki driving?'

'No Madam, but the driver ran away so they killed him.'

I felt my head spin and took a gulp of my drink. 'That's terrible,' I said.

Matthew nodded. 'It is very terrible.'

As we sat in shocked silence I remembered some advice given to us at the Club soon after we arrived saying that we should drive straight on if we had an accident on the road.

Melinda looked confused and tried to pull me out of my chair.

109

'Gail!' she said pointing to the door.

'I promised I would take Melinda to see her friend next door.' I got up. 'Thank you for coming.'

The boys solemnly put their glasses on the table and took their leave.

I took a deep breath and went next door.

'Did you have a nice picnic?' asked Gail's mother.

'It was lovely, thank you. Have you heard about Maliki?'

'No; who's he?'

It always surprised me how little interest she took in the college and I had to keep reminding myself it was different for me as I had worked there for over two years. She listened impassively as I told her about Maliki's murder.

'We came here to get away from the killings in Northern Ireland. But I suppose bad things happen everywhere.'

'I suppose so.' The room became blurred as my eyes filled with tears.

'Are you all right? You've gone quite pale.'

'I feel rather wobbly,' I said in a whisper.

'You'd better go home. Melinda can stay and play, I'll bring her across in half an hour.'

'Thanks, I just need to sit quietly and take in what's happened.'

'Okay.'

I sat on the veranda and tried to focus on our trip out that afternoon. It was a pity we hadn't seen Rebecca but I would see her soon although I knew she would be busy preparing for her exams in June.

I got up and strolled round the garden. A chirruping greeted me as I walked towards a high cage around a banana plant. We had put it up the previous year for the monkey we had rescued from someone who no longer wanted it. 'Hello Biri,' I said as the monkey held out its paw. I scratched the top of its head and recalled how, when we had asked the monkey's name we were told it was Biri. At the time we didn't know that Biri was simply the Hausa

110

word for monkey.

Adrian looked serious when he returned and we talked about the tragic death of Maliki although he didn't have any further information about what happened in Gwoza.

'But I have some news about Rebecca. She's married!'

'Oh! Did you see her?' But I knew that was a silly question.

'She's pregnant and won't be coming back to college.'

'Oh no! What about her exams?'

'She's allowed to take them but not allowed to attend any classes.'

'That's really sad especially as she's so clever. I wonder if that's why the family weren't at home.'

'It could be; her house mistress seemed to think she was staying in Mubi.'

'She mentioned a boyfriend. I hope she's all right. I wonder when the baby's due?'

'If she's in Mubi I'm sure she'll be in touch.'

'I really hope so.'

# Chapter 15    A steep climb to Girimburum

A few days later I was sorting through my research notes when I heard footsteps on the gravel drive. There was a tap on the door.

'Koko!' said a familiar voice.

'Rebecca! How lovely to see you!' For a moment I was taken aback by her new air of confidence as I looked at the young woman before me.

'How are you? Where is Melinda?'

'She's in the garden with Ahmadu. Come.'

We found Melinda splashing her hands in a tub of water that Ahmada was using to wash the clothes.

Melinda squealed in delight when she saw Rebecca who lifted her in the air and I saw a flash of gold on her ring finger.

'I hear that you are married. Congratulations!'

'Yes, I am married.' Rebecca put Melinda down and twiddled her wedding ring thoughtfully.

'We must have some cake to celebrate,' I said and stepped into the kitchen, pleased that I had baked a chocolate cake the day before.

We sat in the shade near the house while Melinda brought various toys to show Rebecca. She said that her husband's name was Sylvester but they were living apart at the moment because he had returned to his college in the south. She looked wistful as she told me she was living with Sylvester's brother's family in Mubi.

'It's a pity you can't be with your parents,' I said thinking of the last few weeks of my pregnancy so far from my husband.

'Mubi is better. I am near the hospital.' Her voice was practical. 'But if you wish to visit my parents we can go. There is a village I want to show you. You can ask questions there.'

'That would be lovely. Where is the village?'

'It is high in the mountain near Sahuda. It is called

112

Girimburum. My father will take us. He is looking forward to seeing you and your husband again.'

We talked about her family and then the conversation turned inevitably to the shocking news of Maliki's death.

'These people from Gwoza. They are not civilised,' said Rebecca.

Although I was slightly taken aback by her attitude, there was no doubting that the killing of an innocent passenger in a car was a crazed act of retribution for knocking down a pedestrian.

'The Gude are peaceful people, she continued. 'Christians, Muslims, Pagans – we all live in harmony with each other.'

I nodded, not trusting myself to speak as I thought of the young art teacher whose life had been snatched so cruelly.

Rebecca bent down to speak to Melinda. 'You will come with your mother when we visit my people?'

Melinda nodded vigorously.

'I'll drive you to your brother-in-law's house then I'll know where to pick you up when we go to see your family.'

***

The following Saturday we set off for Sahuda. Rebecca's brothers were very pleased to see her and her mother promised she would cook a special meal for all of us when we returned from Girimburum.

Pastor Johanna led the way along a path through dry grasses before skirting a settlement at the foot of the mountain. Then the path narrowed and became uneven as it climbed steeply up the mountainside. I was impressed by the ease with which Rebecca strode along chatting to Melinda who was enjoying the ride in her carrier on Adrian's back.

After about thirty minutes we arrived at a small collection of dwellings packed close together on the side of the mountain. We were welcomed warmly by Chief Aliyu and Rugwa, a distinguished looking man with a neat white beard, who was introduced as the Chief's helper. The Chief's compound was smaller than those I had visited in Sahuda and Lamurde. Apart from Rugwa, who wore an indigo caftan and multi-coloured hat, the other men, including Chief Aliyu, wore short white tunics. As was the custom for married Gude women, the Chief's two wives had shaven heads. The senior wife wore a plain calf length wrapper tied above her chest but the younger wife wore hers around her waist.

Despite the eighty-nine inhabitants being mainly Muslim or Pagan, Pastor Johanna was obviously liked and respected. When he explained about my interest in pregnancy and childbirth customs Chief Aliyu said it was important that the traditional ways were remembered. He told us that there are many clans in the Gude tribe but the people in his clan are the same as those in Lamurde. They moved to the mountains because hunting animals for food was better. There was some laughter as Pastor Johanna translated Rugwa's comment that another reason for the move was because some of the younger members of the clan wanted to become chiefs.

Apart from the Chief's two wives who remained standing while the rest of us sat on the ground, I didn't see any women and so I didn't feel able to ask questions about pregnancy. When I asked about childbirth I was told that women went to the health post in Sahuda or travelled to the hospital in Mubi. However, there was a blacksmith's wife in Girimburum who would give local medicine to women experiencing a long labour.

I was unable to get an answer to my question about witchdoctors but whether that was because they did not want to talk about in the Pastor's presence or whether he hadn't been prepared to translate my question, I will never know. However, after some discussion, he told me that some people naturally know about medicines prepared from local plants and fruits used to treat illnesses such as

114

leprosy, gonorrhoea, small pox, chicken pox and 'general weakness of the body.'

I then asked if there were special celebrations after the birth of twins. Chief Aliyu said that, the day after twins are born, two hens are slaughtered and the meat offered to the twins, although it is eaten by their parents. He continued, saying that after seven days a ram is slaughtered and relatives come for a feast. The twins are lain on a grass mat and there is singing and dancing.

I asked if twins receive any special gifts and he said that sometimes two small pots are made and kept in a thatched hut which acts as a shrine. Sacrificial food is cooked in the pots before dawn so that evil spirits won't see the offering. The interpretation took quite a while and it seemed that the Chief was checking that the Pastor was translating exactly what he said.

I wanted to ask if he had any of these special pots he could show me but I could see that Rebecca was becoming uncomfortable.

However, everyone was happy for me to take photos. Chief Aliyu posed, first with himself and Rugwa and then with his wives. Adrian photographed the elders sitting on the ground close together so they could all benefit from the slight shade of a spindly tree. The final portrait was of me standing between Aliyu's wives with the eldest smiling as she held Melinda.

After we had said our farewells we retraced our steps and I was surprised to find ourselves back in Sahuda more quickly than I expected.

Rebecca's mother was obviously delighted to see her daughter and, as usual, made us very welcome. Melinda appeared very much at home as she pottered about and played with the two youngest boys. After our meal, Hajara packed up some food for Rebecca to take to her brother-in-law's family in Mubi. She issued Rebecca some instructions on how to look after herself then clasped my hand, thanked me for bringing her daughter and urged us to come again.

# Chapter 16    The potter's secrets

As I got to know Rebecca better our relationship changed subtly from teacher and student to friends with common interests. Pastor Johanna's house in Sahuda was beginning to feel like a second home and, now that we had the excuse of taking Rebecca to see her family, we visited more frequently. I felt a sense of peace as I watched the children play or helped Rebecca's mother shell groundnuts while feeling the breeze, cooler in this higher altitude, on my bare arms.

However, the peace was shattered on February 13th 1976 when the President, Murtala Muhammed, was assassinated during an ambush while travelling to his office in Lagos. He was only thirty-seven. The government had crushed the coup by the evening but hadn't managed to capture Colonel Dimka and some of the others involved. A government spokesman made a radio announcement that a coup attempt had been crushed and several arrests made. A 6pm to 6am curfew was imposed and all borders and airports were closed. Details of the President's death were officially announced the next day and his deputy, General Obasanjo, was named as his successor. Obasanjo was a Christian and many people felt that the partnership of a Muslim President and Christian deputy had worked well, with both politicians trying to end corruption and religious intolerance.

According to Muslim custom, General Mohammed Murtala's body was flown to Kano and buried in his hometown within 24 hours of his death. Seven days of national mourning were declared. This, and the closure of the borders, proved problematic for boarding schools around the country including our TTC. Some of the students who lived locally returned home but most chose to remain on the college compound where meals were served as usual but there were no lessons. It was a strange and rather worrying time. Some ex-pats took the opportunity to visit Maiduguri. The journey took far longer than usual because there were so many check points manned by soldiers, many armed with machine guns.

I took advantage of the closure of the college to spend some time in Lamurde with Marcus and Ahmed.

Since the visit to Girimburum, I had wanted to find out more about the special god pots that were made when twins were born so we arranged to see the witchdoctor.

I sat in my usual place on the ground next to one of his wives while Awo explained that twins are superior people who have special protection from the gods. He reiterated what Chief Aliyu had told us about the twin's father asking the blacksmith to make two small pots to be kept in a special hut in the compound.

There was an intake of breath from everyone when Awo beckoned me towards a small thatched hut almost hidden against the cornstalk fence surrounding the compound.

I turned to Marcus who nodded so I stood up and walked over to the hut. Marcus and Ahmed remained seated until Awo asked Marcus to join me. Then he opened the door and went inside. Marcus and I bent our heads low but remained in the doorway. At first, it was difficult to see but gradually my eyes became accustomed to the darkness. There was an aromatic scent and when I looked upwards, I saw bunches of herbs hanging from the rafters. In the centre of the room was a wooden table on which lay a couple of small clay pots. Awo pointed to them and explained what they were used for.

'He says that this is where he comes to offer sacrifice to the gods for a good harvest or for people who come to him suffering illness.'

''Does he have any special pots for twins here?' I asked.

I could see Awo shaking his head as Marcus translated the question.

Marcus listened intently as Awo appeared to be telling him to do something.

117

'He says I should ask my mother to make you some twin god pots. You can take them back to England and, if your next confinement is with twins, everything will go well.'

There was laughter when he said this but I knew that I had been honoured to be shown the witchdoctor's shrine.

When we arrived back at Marcus' compound he told his mother what the witchdoctor had said. She seemed pleased and said that she planned to collect clay from the river to make pots the next day so we could come the day after.

\*\*\*

The Nigerian flag at the centre of the primary school assembly and play area was still at half-mast when we drove through Lamurde a couple of days later. Some children were playing football and others wandered aimlessly about, unaccustomed to the unscheduled holiday.

Marcus's little sister was making tiny pots in a shaded part of the compound and Melinda toddled over to join her.

His mother was sitting on the ground surrounded by cooking pots waiting to be fired. In front of her was a large enamel bowl containing the clay and a rudimentary mould made from a wooden block with a depression in the centre the same size as the pots. She scooped a handful of clay and rolled it into a ball then turned it in the mould until it was the shape of a pot. I watched, fascinated, as she formed the lip by hand then carefully trimmed the top with a razor.

'Look, she is going to add the gaze,' said Marcus when his mother picked up a smooth stone and began to burnish the pot.

'What's she doing now?' I asked when she poured something from a smaller enamel bowl over the pot.'

'She is using mahogany oil to make it shine.'

'Those look like baobab seeds,' said Adrian when she picked up a string of large seeds strung together.

'Yes, she uses them to get the final patina.'

The potter paid us no attention as she concentrated on her work.

'These pots are an unusual colour,' I said and knelt down to get a closer look at the yellow pots on the ground.

'They will change when they are fired. They will become,' Marcus paused searching for the correct word.

'Terracotta?' asked Adrian.

'Yes. Terracotta.'

I could see sweat glistening on his mother's bare back as the sun rose higher in the sky.

'It's very hard work,' I said. 'Where are they fired?'

'There's a hollow outside the compound which my mother fills with charcoal and dry grass. She stacks the pots on top then covers them with more dried grass and twigs and sets light to the underneath. She leaves the fire to smoulder till it burns itself out.'

'Don't the pots break in the heat?'

'Not often. She is careful to wait until there is little wind. When the pots are cool she checks them carefully. Then they are ready to sell in the market.'

'So these are all cooking pots?'

'Yes. She will make your twin god pots next time. But,' Marcus added, 'she has to be alone when she makes god pots.' He paused and glanced at Ahmed.

'You will have to negotiate the price. Making these pots is a special skill. It takes a lot of energy,' said Ahmed seriously.

'Of course. We have no idea of the price. You can negotiate for us.'

We did not tell them that we had a particular interest in twins. Adrian's father was the eldest of twins but his brother had been still born.

Marcus's mother put the baobab string aside and held up the pot she had been working on. We all voiced our approval and she gave a broad smile then called to her

119

daughter who brought her a bowl of water to wash her hands.

She turned to us expectantly and Ahmed began the negotiations which proceeded amiably and a price was agreed to our mutual satisfaction.

Ten days later we were the proud owners of four god pots. The larger, more intricate two were for boys and the smaller more rounded pots were for girls.

# Chapter 17    Margaret and other babies

College life returned to normal and, as classes finished earlier on Fridays, I arranged to go to Njairi with Hannatu and Hajara. They took me to meet Aishatu, a young Pagan woman dressed in leaves. She was sitting on the floor of a rudimentary compound holding a sickly looking baby wrapped in a cloth that might once have been white. Sitting next to her was a small boy wearing khaki shorts that were too big for him. Aishatu pointed proudly to the boy and I bent down to greet him. He whispered a reply and I looked questioning at Hannatu.

'He's deaf,' she said.

'Oh!' The sound of children's laughter rang out and I could think of nothing appropriate to say. 'How old is he?' I asked Aishatu.

A conversation followed between the child's mother and the students and I could see the girls appeared shocked.

'The boy is eight years old,' Hajara told me in some disbelief. 'The mother says that two of her children were still-born and one died when it was only two weeks old.'

There was no shade in the compound and I was bathed in sweat as I stood there trying to comprehend the enormity of Aishatu's loss.

'Please tell her I'm sorry,' I said.

Hannatu spoke rapidly but the woman fixed her eyes on the ground and shrugged.

'I think we should leave,' said Hajara quietly.

When we returned to Hananatu's compound her father put out chairs for us to sit on.

I knew that only five of their ten children had survived and wasn't sure how to bring up the subject of multiple infant deaths with Mary. However she appeared calm as she explained the beliefs of her forebears while making clear to me that, since she and her husband had become Christians, they did not share these views. She said that

121

many babies die due to their mother's ignorance and that she had become a village midwife because she wanted to help women during their labour. Over the last few years the number of infant deaths in Njari had decreased due to women having ante-natal checks.

I then broached the subject of Aishatu and her tiny baby and Hannatu and her mother spoke in agitated voices.

'She says she begged her to go to the hospital,' said Hannatu.

With her daughter translating, Mary, went on to tell me that the traditional Gude belief is that many babies die because God didn't bring them here to stay, just to look and go back again. She said that sometimes women harbour an evil spirit that causes her children to die.

When I asked if there was any way to prevent this happening she said:

*The pregnant woman goes with a village elder to the tree or stream where the spirit lives and the old man begs the spirit not to return. When the child is born no razor blade will touch its head till it is seven years old and then it will not die. A sheep is killed and a leg given to the old man for his help in driving away the evil spirit.'*

Remembering Chinua's Achebe's acclaimed novel, 'Things Fall Apart', I asked Mary if what she had told me was similar to Obange children described in the book. Obange is an Igbo word meaning 'children come and go' and refers to the belief that the same child keeps returning.

Mary denied this, saying that Igbo customs were different from those practised by traditional Gude who believe it is not the same child who returns.

***

When I dropped the girls back at the secondary school it seemed strange that our friends were no longer living there. It would have been lovely to call in on Adelchi and talk about everything I had seen and heard.

Instead I called on the Polish doctor at the hospital and

told her briefly about my research. She was interested and arranged for me to be shown round the maternity unit by a senior midwife. The midwife was wary of me at first but, once she realised that I wasn't there in an official capacity, she was pleased to show me the facilities.

We had a quick look at the delivery ward which was much smaller than the English equivalent but seemed to be well equipped.

She told me that there was an ante-natal clinic every Thursday and post-natal every Friday. I was familiar with the post-natal clinic as I had taken Melinda there for her vaccinations.

After visiting the maternity unit the senior midwife took me to the doctors' office where the Polish doctor was happy to answer my questions.

She said that women often arrived at the hospital in the middle of a difficult labour. It upset her that sometimes women came too late and they were unable to save the baby's life. The doctor shook her head as she told me how simple hygiene practices during childbirth could have prevented many of the complications she saw. I knew that the cord was cut with a razor or a sharpened corn stalk but had not realised that more infections were caused by razors which were sometimes rusty whereas corn stalks were disposable.

I was about to ask another question when an orderly tapped on the door and told the doctor she was needed urgently. I thanked her for her time as she apologised and hurried away.

\*\*\*

A few days later we went to see Kitty and Dick and they told us that the wife of one of the trainee pastors had recently died in childbirth. The grief-stricken young father had no idea how to look after the baby but did not want to leave it in the care of relatives far away. For the first few weeks a couple of mothers who were breast-feeding their own babies suckled the motherless infant. Then Kitty stepped in and showed the man how to mix formula milk and bottle feed the baby. She told me that she showed him how to wash the bottle after each feed but she didn't teach him to sterilise the bottle as clean boiled water was precious and using sterilising fluid incorrectly could harm the child.

The incident made me realise I hadn't seen Yakubu's wife and baby recently so I went to the servants' quarter as soon as we got back.

'They are well, Madam. How are you?' Yakubu answered my question impassively.

I noticed Ahmadu shake his head as I replied in the traditional way. A faint cry came from inside the room and I felt suddenly fearful.

'And your baby? How is your baby?' I tried to keep my voice calm.

'The baby will be well. She has medicine.'

'What sort of medicine?' I asked anxiously.

'Quranic medicine.'

I frowned and turned to Ahmadu whose English was more fluent than Yakubu's.

'It is medicine from the Imam. He uses Quranic ink to write a healing verse from the Holy Quran on a slate. Then he washes it off and the person drinks the holy water.

'What's wrong with the baby?'

'She shit too much.' Ahmadu's face was impassive.

'Have you taken her to hospital?'

'No Madam.' Ahmadu answered for his friend. 'The Imam is giving her medicine.'

'May I see the baby?'

An agitated conversation followed before Yakubu opened the door slightly and I peered into the fetid air where his wife was sitting on the floor rocking her daughter. She looked like a new born baby but I knew she was several months old.

I forced myself to greet the woman calmly. This was different from my visit to Aishatu. Yakubu had worked for us for two years and I felt a responsibility to his family.

'I would like to take you to see the doctor at the hospital,' I said.

A look of relief mixed with fear crossed her face as she looked at her husband.

'We will go soon,' I said firmly.

I heard raised voices as I left but one look at the child told me I needed to act quickly.

I explained the situation to Adrian and fifteen minutes later we both went to talk to Yakubu who was still undecided.

'Many of our students are Muslims,' Adrian said gently, 'but when they are ill they go to the hospital for medicine and they get better.'

Yakubu's wife stood in the doorway, holding her tiny baby wrapped in a clean cloth. She inclined her head and took a step forward.

'I think she is ready,' I said.

Yakubu helped his wife and daughter to the car and the three of them sat in the back as I drove carefully to the hospital.

'You should have come earlier.' The doctor looked sternly at the couple after she had examined the child and prescribed anti-biotics. 'She is severely dehydrated and needs to be admitted.'

I didn't dare form the question I wanted to ask the doctor about the child's chances but she must have known what I was thinking.

'She will be put on a saline drip in the children's ward. The mother will stay with her daughter. You can check her condition in the morning.' She gave me a weary smile as we left.

I stayed with Yakubu and his wife until their daughter was laid in a cot and attached to a drip. As I left, I waved aside Yakubu's assurances that he would be at work in the next day.

The following morning there was a tap on the kitchen door.

'My daughter has passed, Madam,' said Yakubu gravely and left before I could say anything.

Melinda was puzzled and then distressed when I picked her up and sobbed.

'Let's go and see Gail,' I said when I had dried my eyes.

My neighbour had just received letters from home and I sat, half listening as she talked about her family in Ireland while the girls played on the veranda.

*** 

The birth of Rebecca's daughter was a happy event. She was born at the end of March in Mubi hospital. Her brother came with the news and asked me to take him to fetch their mother from Sahuda.

I strapped Melinda in her car seat with a bottle of juice and we set off.

'Have you come from Sahuda?' I asked the young man sitting beside me.

'No, Madam. I am staying with a relative in Mubi. I will start secondary school soon,' he added proudly.

'Your parents must be proud of you,' I said keeping my eyes on the road.

'Yes, I shall work hard and then I will train to be a doctor.'

'I wish you well.' I smiled at him then turned my attention to the road ahead.

There had been no rain for five months and the road surface was hard packed which made driving relatively easy until I found myself behind a lorry which trailed clouds of dust, making it difficult to see. As the road wound uphill to Sahuda Melinda began to get fidgety.

'We're nearly there,' I said as I put the car into first gear and, keeping my distance from the lorry, drove cautiously up the hill.

Suddenly another lorry appeared over the brow. I slammed my foot on the brake and watched in horror as the lorry in front of me swerved off the road and bumped along the rough ground. The oncoming lorry hardly slowed down but, as it careered past me, I was just able to see the brightly painted slogan on the front - In God We Trust.

'Bloody idiot!' I yelled.

'Idyot!' shouted Melinda gleefully.

'Sorry,' I said to my passenger who looked shocked but whether it was from the near miss or my language I couldn't tell.

'You are a good driver, Madam,' he said judiciously.

My heart was thumping as I drove slowly into the village. Rebecca's parents were coming to meet us. I parked the car and the Pastor told me that they had already received a message that Rebecca had delivered in the night.

Rebecca's mother was dressed in her best clothes and her face was wreathed in smiles. She was holding an overnight bag and a basket of vegetables that I guessed were freshly picked from their farm.

Her son got out of the car and, after an exchange of greetings, held open the door for his mother and thanked me for the lift.

'Aren't you coming back with us?' I asked.

'No, Madam. I will stay and look after my younger brothers. Thank you for helping my sister.'

'You are welcome,' I smiled.

Melinda was clamouring to get out but I could see that Hajara was eager to see her daughter and granddaughter so I drank some water from the cooler, gave Melinda a biscuit and topped up her juice. She was delighted when Hajara got in the seat next to her and prattled happily most of the way back to Mubi.

I dropped Hajara at the hospital and went home with a promise to visit in the afternoon.

Melinda helped me sort through some of her baby clothes and wrap them in tissue paper. After lunch I drove into town with the clothes and bought some Johnson's baby lotion for the baby and talcum powder for Rebecca then continued to the hospital and parked on some rough ground near the entrance. Traders were offering cooked food, fruit and soft drinks while women were squatting round small fires cooking food for their relatives. People were also selling empty bottles because medicine was rarely dispensed in bottles but poured into containers provided by the patients and their relatives.

I paused in the doorway of the maternity ward. Rebecca was sitting nursing her baby and waved when she saw me. There was just enough room to make my way along the neat rows of cots to where Rebecca and a couple of other mothers were sitting at the end of the ward.

'You look well,' I said.

'I am well,' Rebecca replied, her face glowing as she handed me the baby.

'She's beautiful,' I murmured as I inhaled her sweet new born scent and gently stroked her cheek. 'Does she have a name yet?'

'Not officially till after the naming ceremony but I shall call her Margaret.'

I looked around and could see that not all the women looked as radiant as Rebecca.

'No problems then?' I asked.

Rebecca shook her head. 'She came quickly.'

'How did you get here?' I gently put the baby back in Rebecca's arms and leant against the wall for support.

'My brother-in-law sent for a taxi. You know his house is not far from here.'

'And where is your mother?'

'She is buying some food.'

'How long will you stay here?'

'Just this night. My father will arrange a car to take us to Sahuda tomorrow. That is the custom with the first born, to stay with the mother's family. We will have our own house before the next one comes,' she said confidently.

I knew that one of the reasons for the new mother

128

returning to her parents was that keeping her apart from her husband was a good contraceptive.

'Melinda wanted you to have these,' I said and took the clothes from my bag. 'And these are from me,' I added as I handed her the toiletries.

She thanked me and we both sat in silence, exhausted after the events of the day. In fact I felt totally worn out and could hardly keep my eyes open. I found myself swaying and held on to Rebecca's chair for support.

'Are you all right?' Rebecca looked worried.

I gave a secret smile as I looked down at Margaret nuzzling her mother's breast. 'I will be fine.'

Rebecca's face searched mine. 'I think you are under state.'

I nodded. 'You may be right but it could be the heat.'

'Have you told your husband?'

'Yes, but no one else. It's too early to be sure. Please don't mention it to anyone.'

'It will be our secret!' Rebecca said conspiratorially. 'Now you must go and rest.'

'I'll wait till your mother comes.'

Hajara returned a few minutes later and I left with promises to see her again soon.

# Chapter 18   Mambilla is too far

When Clive and Adelchi told us about their transfer to Gembu we promised we would visit them in the Easter holidays.

March was particularly hot that year and we were suffering from a lack of fresh vegetables. I developed a sty on my eye lid and boils were commonplace. We were feeling listless in the heat and the thought of cool mountain scenery was enticing despite what we knew would be an arduous journey to the Mambilla Plateau.

I was torn between seeing another part of Nigeria or staying in Mubi to learn more about the customs of the Mandara villages, especially as it was possible I shared a secret with the mothers I had spoken to about the early days of pregnancy.

However, we were looking forward to seeing Adelchi and Clive and so to make the journey easier we offered a lift to Nelson, a fifth form student who lived on the Plateau.

The first day was long and fraught with difficulties. I am normally excited by river crossings but had not expected the River Benue to be so wide and the crossing so precarious. We waited a long time in a queue of overcrowded lorries on a dirt road leading to the ferry near Yola. When it was our turn to move we bumped up the wooden ramp of pontoons lashed together and on to the ferry. Melinda was afraid of the shouting and revving engines but, once the ferry was moving slowly across the river, we were all fascinated by the fishermen in canoes casting their nets into the water. Screwing up our eyes against the sun we glimpsed flashes of silver from fish caught in the nets. The crossing took about fifteen minutes but disembarkation the other side threatened to be a free-for-all till we, along with the other cars, were waved onto the rocky verge and crawled past the lorries.

Vendors were selling fruit and cooked food but we

drove on until we found shade to park under and had some of the refreshments we had brought. It was good to stretch our legs but the relentless heat from the sun made us pleased to get back into the car. The road became increasingly pot-holed and our exhaust pipe fell off before we reached the rest house in Jalingo. Adrian managed to tie it back on with wire and Nelson knew someone in Jalingo who made it more secure.

We were lucky we had a passenger who knew the local area although unfortunately he did not speak much English and paid no attention to our voluble daughter.

We were up early the following morning and, after a slow two hundred and fifty two kilometre drive, we crossed the River Taraba and began our ascent into the Highlands. According to our Michelin map the next ninety-three kilometres was appropriately marked as a Picturesque Route. After the dusty flat lands of the Benue plain the lush vegetation and cooler air gave us a new lease of life.

'How's she bearing up?' I asked Adrian as he put our Renault 12 into the lowest gear to cope with a sudden rocky patch.

'She's doing fine, it's a good job I upgraded the shock absorbers.'

'Just look at that view!' I pointed at the mountain peaks to the east as we climbed higher.

For the first time since leaving Mubi, our passenger looked animated as he turned to speak to me.

'This is my home country.'

'It's beautiful,' I said although I felt awed by the vastness surrounding us and began to understand some of Clive and Adelchi's trepidation about being posted to such a remote area.

The sun disappeared and storm clouds filled the sky but Nelson was unperturbed. By the time we reached Serti it was raining steadily and the car slithered on muddy ground as we left the road and parked in the centre of the village. I was surprised to see some of our students lounging under a corrugated shelter outside a bar. Melinda had fallen asleep so, much as I wanted to stretch my legs, I simply wound down the window and called a greeting. Several came and shook my hand, expressing admiration mixed with concern that we were continuing to Gembu. Not for the first time that day I wondered if we had made the right decision and I felt suddenly queasy. I glanced at the Michelin map and comforted myself that we only had another ninety kilometres to our destination.

Melinda woke up soon after the rain stopped so we pulled off the road and got out to stretch our legs and have a drink and some biscuits.

All around us were mountains. Unlike the familiar Mandara around Mubi, these were higher and the valleys steeper, appearing infinite as they stretched east across the Cameroons into the Central African Republic. A woman bearing a basket of wood on her back paused to look at us. We greeted her in Hausa but she shook her head uncomprehendingly. Tightly packed wooden branches stuck out of the basket about a metre above the woman's head and I wondered how she was able to walk with such a load, let alone up such steep slopes. A little further on we saw a younger woman with a smaller basket which had an axe sticking casually out of the top.

'Baby!' shouted Melinda and pointed to the woman as we drove past.

'Oh she's carrying it on her front,' I said and waved to the young woman who had a baby strapped to her chest with a brightly coloured cloth.

For an instant I was reminded of Scotland as we passed an area covered with conifers. We rounded another bend and saw cattle grazing on lush grass. Unlike the thin beasts we were used to seeing these were fat and sleek.

The sky was turning a blood red and I glanced at my watch. 'I hope we make it before dark,' I murmured.

Adrian said nothing but drove as fast as he dared. My stomach lurched as we hit a rock in the road but Melinda was wide-eyed with excitement at the thought of seeing

Helen and Philip again. We reached Gembu just as the sun was setting and followed Clive's directions to the secondary school. I felt immeasurable relief when we came to a halt outside their house set in a garden of mature trees and flowering shrubs.

The welcome we received made up for the journey.

\*\*\*

We had a comfortable night's sleep and woke the next morning feeling surprisingly refreshed. Although it was the holidays, Clive and Adelchi had a few things to do at school and we suggested we took the children for a walk. Clive pointed out a path going through some woods.

'It's a nice little round walk,' he said.

Five year old Helen proudly led the way with her little brother close behind.

'Are you sure this is the right way?' I asked as the narrow path led steeply downhill.

'It's along there,' she said pointing to a track leading round the side of the hill. But Philip was already running past her so Adrian hoisted Melinda on his shoulders and we hurried after him down the steep slope.

'Listen!' said Adrian when we had caught up. 'Can you hear that bird?'

'It's telling us to go back', I laughed as we heard the familiar call of a guinea fowl, sometimes known as the go-back bird due to its insistent call.

There was a scrambling in the undergrowth and at the side of the path were a pair of black guinea fowl with their distinctive pink necks bent low as they pecked the ground for food.

'Can we find their nest?' asked Philip.

'Maybe, if you're very quiet,' said Adrian.

I felt a stabbing pain and clutched my stomach. 'We don't want to disturb them,' I said firmly and turned round.

'All right kids, shall we find that other path?' Adrian

looked at me questioningly as he turned round.

I found it increasingly difficult to keep up with the children as they skipped ahead and I was convinced they were heading in the wrong direction. The magnificent scenery we had seen from the car was proving challenging to walk in.

***

When we arrived back at the house I was shaking with exhaustion but, apart from needing a drink, the three children were fine and settled down to play in the shady garden.

Adlechi came back soon afterwards and I offered to help her prepare the meal but she had brought a young relative from her home town to help with the chores and I welcomed the opportunity to sit quietly.

Over lunch we continued our conversation from the night before and caught up on the gossip from Mubi as well hearing about how they were settling into life in Gembu.

'Supplies are difficult,' said Adelchi.

'But the climate is good for crops.' Clive was more enthusiastic. 'We have a good gardener and he has already planted potatoes, tomatoes, spinach and beans as well as maize. And we have got to know someone who runs a tea plantation. He is always interested in showing people round so we'll take you there.'

'Can we take Melinda to the beach?' asked Helen.

'The beach?' Adrian and I both asked at once.

'She means the river; it's the boundary between Nigeria and Cameroon but there's a sandy beach on this side and the children love to paddle.'

'And we made a dam,' said Philip proudly.

'I will make us a picnic and we can go there when you are rested.' Adelchi looked at me quizzically.

After lunch Clive offered to take us on a tour of the school but I excused myself and went to lie down.

'Are you all right?' Adrian looked shocked when he found me sitting on the edge of the bed a couple of hours later.

'I think I've had a miscarriage,' I whimpered.

I have only a vague recollection of the next few days. Apart from the embarrassment of being ill in someone else's house, I was grieving the loss of my unborn child. I knew that miscarriages were a fact of life for women in Nigeria and they were expected to get over them quickly. Although they were less common in my own culture they were still a taboo subject and Adrian and Clive tiptoed nervously about asking me if there was anything I needed.

'Mambilla is too far, the road is not good. And our families are far away.' Adlechi shook her head as she brought me some supper.

The next day Adrian gave me a tonic he bought from a small shop that sold pharmaceuticals. It was called Bull's Blood. I don't know if it was the tonic or the enforced rest but I recovered my strength enough to enjoy our holiday in Mambilla.

\*\*\*

Eighteen months later we were able to return our friends' hospitality when they came to stay with us in Lincolnshire. Melinda was three and our baby daughter, Emily, was two months old.

# Chapter 19  Invitation to a naming ceremony

Helen and Keith called to see us as soon as we got back, eager to hear news of how Adelchi and Clive were settling down in Mambilla.

'What's been happening here?' I asked after we'd given an upbeat version of our trip with no mention of my miscarriage.

'Oyeyipo's wife had another baby yesterday. The naming ceremony's next week,' said Helen.

'Everyone's invited, it's at six o'clock in the morning,' added Keith.

'Gosh! That's early; where is it?' asked Adrian.

'In their compound so that'll be no trouble for us as we live next door.'

'I don't suppose it will last long as it's a school day. I guess it'll be all right to bring Melinda. The Oyeyipo children are always friendly when we stop for a chat.'

'You'll have to take notes,' joked Keith.

'I don't think that would be appropriate but it'll be interesting to see the difference as the Oyeyipos are Yoraba. Back in February Rebecca took me to a naming ceremony in Lamurde which started at five o'clock in the evening.'

'Were they one of your Pagan families?'

'No they were Christian,' I replied quietly, sensing his ambivalence about my research.

Helen shot a warning glance at Keith. 'Was it interesting?' she asked.

'It went on rather a long time; I was impressed with how well-behaved the children were. The men sat on one side of the compound and the women on the other but Rebecca and I had to sit with the men.' I paused as I remembered feeling slightly embarrassed about being treated differently from the other women who had been busy cooking when we arrived.

'Didn't the parents and godparents stand together at the front?'

'That's what I expected but Soraya, the mother, sat in the middle of the women and gave the baby to her helper to hold. We all stood up and sang a hymn then sat down for a prayer. One of the pastors read from the Bible and another told a long story about a husband and wife who couldn't agree on the child's name. Then Pastor Bullus held the baby and officially named him Kefus which apparently means rock.'

'I wonder why he wasn't given a name from the Bible as it was led by a pastor?'

'He wasn't given one at the ceremony although I know that some names aren't said aloud but whispered in the child's ear. Anyway, the Pastor charged the parents with giving him a Christian upbringing then there was a prayer and another hymn and we were told we could donate something if we wished.'

'And was that the end of the ceremony?'

'Sweets and kola nuts were handed out and then the food was served but we didn't stay for that.' I paused. 'But something strange happened before that. Throughout the ceremony two women were holding a cloth pretending it was another baby called Kefus.'

'Why would they do that?'

'Rebecca didn't know but the Pastor didn't like it and told them off but they said it was only a bit of fun and they kept hold of the pretend baby. Actually***' I paused as I remembered what I had read about spirit children, 'Maybe it was to protect the real Kefus from dying in infancy.'

There was silence as Keith's scepticism filled the air.

'Well, it'll be interesting to see what happens at a Yoruba naming ceremony,' said Adrian.

***

As it happened, Melinda slept late the morning of the naming ceremony so Adrian left before us and by the time we arrived the party was in full swing. Melinda jiggled to the music as we entered the Oyeyipo's compound and I inhaled the unmistakeable scent of roasting goat. A Yoruba friend of the Oyeyipos who worked at the Secondary School was officiating. Adrian told me afterwards that part of the ceremony had involved putting a tiny piece of chilli pepper on the tip of the baby's tongue.

Everyone was splendidly dressed and many of the women had extravagant headscarves. I was glad I was wearing my Nigerian dress with its exquisite embroidery on the neck and sleeves.

All the teaching staff had been invited and, since the expansion of the college two years previously, this included a lot of younger Nigerian teachers who were very happy to join the early morning celebrations. I was offered a plateful of goat's meat but, when I tentatively took a mouthful, the hot pepper sauce threatened to burn my mouth and I grabbed a glass of something that looked like water. I have never been a fan of neat gin and it is not a beverage I would recommend with breakfast. However, not wishing to give offence, I drank it. I was less circumspect with the goat and passed my plate to a couple of children who were delighted with it and offered some to Melinda who had squatted down next to them. She tentatively put her finger out then shook her head.

I made my way to the table where Mr and Mrs Oyeyipo were sitting and offered my congratulations then looked in some consternation at the bowl full of naira notes of different denominations.

'Don't worry, Mrs Rosser, your husband has given a generous donation,' said Mr Oyeyipo. He smiled, 'I hope you and your daughter are enjoying the party.'

'Yes, very much,' I said. 'But not as wildly as some of the guests,' I thought as I glanced at Adrian, Keith and a group of young teachers laughing uproariously.

In the distance the school bell announced the beginning of lessons and people slowly began to drift away.

'How was teaching?' I asked when Adrian came home

138

at break time.

'Very relaxed,' he replied with a grin.

# Chapter 20    Festival in Lamurde Wamngo

Delighted with our twin god pots, we had asked Marcus if his mother could make us a finial like the one we had seen on Chief Ardo's house. He said that they required special knowledge but he could introduce us to a woman in Lamurde who was skilled in these things. We visited her just before our trip to Mambilla and ordered two finials.

A few days after the naming ceremony, Marcus called to tell me that they were ready to collect.

'Thank you for letting me know. Can you spare the time to accompany us on Sunday morning?

Marcus looked surprised. 'It is certain I can come. Your interest in our culture is very important. I think you would like to visit Awo also?'

'That would be good, there are some more things I would like to ask him.'

There had been a light rain early on Sunday morning and the air felt fresh as we drove off the main road and into Lamurde. Marcus directed us towards the potter's compound and we parked under a silk cotton tree.

'Wait here,' said Marcus. 'I will tell her we have come.'

Ahmed remained with us and explained that the woman would see us outside her compound as she didn't welcome strangers inside.

'That sounds reasonable,' I said. 'We've been fortunate to be invited into so many people's homes.'

Ahmed nodded and smiled at Melinda who was sitting on the ground gathering balls of white fluffy kapok that had fallen from the tree. 'It is because of your daughter; people like to welcome small children.' He paused and thought for a minute. 'I think it is also that you are quiet and you do not thrust your camera in their face.'

I was pleased with the compliment but years later I wished I had taken more photographs.

Marcus came out of the compound with an elderly

woman who, after we had exchanged greetings, placed a grass mat on the ground.

'She will bring the finials now,' said Marcus.

Adrian and I looked at each other in anticipation. A few minutes later the woman carefully placed a finial on the mat. There was no mistaking it had been made for a man's hut. It stood about one metre high and consisted of a large pot standing on a circular base around which were animals and a warrior sporting an unfeasibly large phallus. On top of the pot was a shallow dish painted white. Without a word she returned to her compound and brought out the second finial. It also stood on a base and had a shallow dish on top. However, there were no representations of animals or people on this; instead it was decorated with rounded shapes to represent femininity and fertility.

'They are very impressive,' said Adrian as he bent down to examine them.

'There're amazing.' I agreed feeling somewhat stunned by what we had commissioned.

Marcus shook his head. 'I have never seen one like this before,' he pointed to the male finial.

'We must pack them carefully,' said Ahmed.

'We've brought blankets to wrap them in.'

There was a rapid exchange between Marcus and the woman and he asked us if we were satisfied. We said that we were very pleased and I handed over the money which she quickly counted then shifted her wrapper to cover her chest and tucked the naira notes between her breasts.

When the finials were carefully packed in the car boot Adrian drove slowly to the foot of Lamurde Mountain. The rough track felt familiar now and we soon reached Awo's ramshackle compound perched on the side of the hill.

He was decorating a small stool he had carved from a single piece of wood similar to one I had bought from Mubi Market as a gift for my goddaughter. He sat on the ground and dipped a metal rod into a small hollow of burning charcoal which he used to burn criss-cross

141

patterns in the wood.

Melinda squatted next to one of Awo's relatives who was holding a baby about six months old. Melinda held out a piece of fluff from the silk cotton tree and everyone laughed when the baby reached out for it.

Marcus explained that we would be returning to England soon and Awo's son asked when we would come back. I was about to say I hoped to return sometime in the future when there was the familiar 'Koko!' outside the compound and Chief Ardo arrived.

When he heard we were leaving he turned to Marcus and said something that appeared to surprise him.

'The Chief is inviting you to the harvest festival at the end of the month. He says you will be his welcome guests.'

I caught the look of amazement on Ahmed's face and, realising that this was an honour, I thanked the Chief and said I was looking forward to it very much.

The Chief appeared to give instructions to Marcus then, not wanting to intrude on his visit to Awo, we took our leave.

We walked in single file back down the track but when we reached the car I asked Marcus and Ahmed about the festival.

'It is for Pagans,' said Ahmed. 'They do not like anyone from outside to see.'

Marcus shook his head. 'They don't mind Gude like us who registered as Muslims when we went to school.'

'It will be a privilege,' I said as I got into the car.

***

In those last few weeks Rebecca and her baby were frequent visitors to our house. They came one afternoon when Melinda was sitting in the shade of the banana plant chatting to our monkey who gibbered back.

The dry season was over and Yakubu was threshing the rice we had planted. The agricultural department had asked us if we would plant a variety of rice that grows in dry climates in order to show people who passed our house on their way to market that it was possible to cultivate rice in the Mandara. We agreed and they gave us the seed and sent someone with a tractor to prepare the ground. Yakubu did the planting, harvesting and threshing.

'You have a good rice crop,' said Rebecca when I had brought us some cool drinks and she had settled down to feed her baby.

'Yes, tomorrow, Yakubu's wife will separate the grain from the chaff. I will give you some when it is ready.'

Rebecca looked wistful. 'Are you looking forward to going back to England?'

'I'm looking forward to seeing my family but I'll miss everyone here.'

'We will write to each other.'

'Of course we will; you must let me know your new address.'

'Yes, Sylvester and I will be together when he has finished his studies.'

In the distance the college bell sounded for the four o'clock assembly.

'Is Mr Rosser in his laboratory?'

'No, he went to Yola yesterday to get our leaving documents sorted. He should be back soon.'

'It feels strange that there is no longer a North East State,' said Rebecca.

'Yes, I can't get used to writing Gongola State as my address. And the road to Yola isn't as easy as the new road to Maiduguri.'

'Murtala Mohammed promised to make more states; it's good that the Government is doing what he wanted. They say it is better for Nigeria to have more states, the others were too big.'

'I'm sure it will be better; I just hope that all our documents got transferred from Maiduguri.'

Rebecca placed Margaret on the mat where Melinda was building a tower with her blocks and we talked about our hopes and dreams for their futures.

'I suppose I should go,' said Rebecca reluctantly. 'I am going to Sahuda next week. You must visit me there.'

'Thank you, it will be good to see your parents again.'

Melinda and I walked with her to the road and I watched her striding confidently down the hill with her baby on her back.

Adrian arrived soon afterwards and parked in the shade.

'How was the journey?' I asked.

'It was all right and I got quite a lot done despite the chaos.'

Melinda was clamouring for his attention and it wasn't until later that Adrian told me about his trip.

He said that the new offices were not yet ready and the officials he needed to see had their desks set up under shade trees outside buildings that held the government files but were too small to accommodate all the staff.

'I felt sorry for those having to re-locate,' he said. 'Maiduguri temperatures are high but Yola has to cope with ninety per cent humidity as well.'

'I hope they get something sorted before the rains become heavy.'

'Labourers are putting up zinc sheds as a temporary measure. Anyway I didn't have any hassle. I have to go back for our travel vouchers just before we leave.'

***

There was little time to think about the future as I was busy making last visits to people and places that had become part of my life during a momentous four years.

Probably the most memorable experience was our visit to the festival in Lamurde. It was due to start at dusk but the Chief had asked us to arrive before then. We decided it wouldn't be appropriate to take Melinda but she enjoyed visiting Helen and Keith and their chickens and they were happy to look after her.

We left with Marcus and Ahmed straight after roll call

and drove through Mubi, passing considerably more cars than when we had first arrived. Lamurde had also expanded and there were new houses with zinc roofs near the Mubi road.

As usual, we parked outside Marcus's parents' compound and walked to a part of Lamurde Wamngo I didn't recognise until Marcus explained that this area on the side of the mountain had been cleared of grass and shrubs which made it appear unfamiliar.

Before we had a chance to find Chief Ardo, we were greeted formally by a man we hadn't met before and escorted to a round hut on the edge of the clearing. We were ushered inside and the door was closed. After I had become accustomed to the semi-darkness I saw that men in white caftans and turbans of different colours were seated on the floor around the room. I felt Marcus stiffen as he sat down on the earth floor beside me. Adrian and Ahmed were sitting opposite us. There was silence and I could see the whites of Ahmed's eyes as he looked across at Marcus then they both lowered their eyes to the ground. I generally don't feel comfortable in enclosed spaces but I didn't believe that any harm was going to come to us especially as the men's silence felt neutral rather than hostile.

There was a muttering when another man joined the group and looked intently in my direction then nodded as some explanation was given. I was beginning to feel restless when suddenly the door was flung open and a man I recognised appeared. It was the Chief's emissary. He was wearing a pale blue caftan and had a drum slung over one shoulder. He looked surprised to see us and fired questions at Marcus then turned angrily to the man who had brought us to the hut. I looked across at Adrian and we both smiled in relief. A couple of minutes later we were standing outside and I felt a sense of being part of something unfathomable as I looked up at the sky which was now streaked in hues of red and gold.

'What was that all about?' Adrian asked.

Ahmed shrugged. 'They thought you were missionaries.'

There was no time to dwell on the incident as the emissary led us towards the Chief.

He was sitting on a rock near a tree in the centre of the clearing and wearing an extravagant orange turban tied around his head. His indigo robe was embossed with rectangular shapes, over which was a white tunic overlaid with geometric symbols in black. After welcoming us, Chief Ardo said we must take as many photographs as we wanted.

Below the rock were three chairs and the emissary indicated we should sit. He left us and we watched as more and more people arrived. The emissary returned with four young dancers dressed for the ceremony. He indicated that we could take photos and we got up and greeted the girls who were aged about twelve or thirteen. They had closely cropped hair and wore colourful bead aprons around their waists which were fringed with cowrie shells. Bunches of fresh green leaves covered their buttocks and they were bare chested. Around their necks were bead necklaces and shell pendants and they wore bangles made of bronze and bone around their wrists. They all wore sandals and some of the girls were holding small handbags and coloured umbrellas that I had recently seen for sale in Mubi market. The emissary explained that these showed they came from wealthy families. Led by an elderly woman wearing a new wrapper, they danced in front of us and we took photos.

I looked up and noticed that the red sky had turned pink and the full moon was beginning to rise. It was then that the drumming began. The girls and elders of the tribe took their places around the tree and Chief Ardo walked slowly round them holding his caftan as if he was about to curtsey. Then he returned to his seat on the rock and the dancing continued.

On the inside of the circle the men danced slowly due to the weight of the many caftans they were wearing. The girls on the outside were joined by women with shaven heads and their bodies shining with mahogany oil coloured with red ochre. Some of the women carried tins filled with the oil to replenish their make-up. Many of them had babies on their backs in goat skin slings which were also stained in mahogany and ochre.

The dancing continued for about an hour and more and more people came to watch but only 'leaf people' as they were sometimes called joined in the dancing. Marcus told us that they came from isolated villages and quite a few of them were Fali as they were closely connected to the Gude. When they stopped dancing they stood under a tree and the Chief prayed to the gods for a good harvest. Instead of saying Amen everyone cheered and the dancing continued.

We left when the dancing was in full swing but as I glanced at the people watching I noticed some of our students on the side-lines and they appeared to be jeering.

\*\*\*

Our final visit to Lamurde was in our last week. We had been busy packing and decided to give our garden chairs to Chief Ardo.

Melinda toddled in front as we walked up the rough track for the last time; Adrian, Marcus and Ahmed each carrying a folding chair. I found it hard to believe that we had only known Ardo, Awo and their families for just over a year. Half way up we stopped for Adrian to take a photograph and I took a deep breath as I tried to commit the scene to memory. The brown and grey hues of the dry season had given way to vibrant greens. Some acacia trees had brown seed pods hanging down that reminded me of runner beans.

'Are they edible?' I asked.

'Farmers harvest them to feed to their cattle,' said Marcus.

We heard voices and two of the Chief's children caught up with us. They were carrying buckets of water on their heads but did not appear to be out of breath as they asked about the chairs Adrian and the students were carrying.

We continued our ascent and stopped outside the Chief's compound. As always the area outside was freshly swept. Next to the stone mortar were several grinding stones which Melinda attempted to pick up.

As I perched on a low boulder I heard the chuckling call of a laughing dove then looked up at a black kite soring high above the compound.

Chief Ardo was pleased to see us and thanked us gravely for the gift of the chairs. However, he was even more pleased with the photograph we gave of him sitting on his rock. I had taken the colour slide on our first visit and had a copy made when we were on leave.

We talked about the recent festival and asked if the tradition would continue. The Chief shook his head sadly and said that his sons had different ideas now they were at a secondary school run by Roman Catholic priests. He added that, with universal primary education, traditional religions would probably die out in ten years.

He asked if I had any more questions but I felt a lump in my throat and couldn't think of anything. I thanked him for everything and promised to keep in touch via Marcus.

As we began to make our way down the mountain I could feel the Chief's eyes on us until we were out of sight.

Marcus's parents were busy as usual when we arrived. His father greeted us but continued shaping a shaft he was making for an axe head. His mother was polishing a large water pot ready to sell in the market. She put down her cloth when she saw Melinda and marvelled at how much she had grown since our last visit.

I took one last photo then, on the spur of the moment, handed my instamatic camera to Marcus.

'This is for you to carry on taking photographs. I put a new film in yesterday. When you have finished the film you can post it to me and I will have them printed and send them to you. It would be good if you can take some more pictures of farming and any local customs that I can keep and put with my other pictures.'

148

There was a stunned expression of delight on Marcus's face as Adrian added, 'We will give you money for postage.'

His father put down his knife and came to look at the camera in his son's hand and Marcus's brother hurried over from the other side of the compound.

'Everyone is very happy,' said Ahmed who was also smiling broadly.

I showed Marcus how to use the camera and he took a photo of us all.

'I will send you many photos for you to remember us,' said Marcus.

True to his word I received a reel of film three months later.

# Chapter 21    Gifts from the Mandara

The next day we made our last visit to Sahuda.

Melinda helped me sort out some of her clothes to give to Margaret which we put in a basket with a rattle and a toy drum. After lunch we set off along the familiar road climbing south-east towards the Cameroon border.

'My father is at his farm by the dam. I'll send my little brother to tell him you are here,' said Rebecca when we arrived.

'We don't want to interrupt him,' I said. 'Maybe we can see him there.'

'He will be pleased to see you and show you his crops.' Rebecca tied Margaret firmly on her back and took Melinda's hand.

As always, I felt a sense of peace as we followed the path down to the little farm by the river. The late afternoon sun lit up the dam's sandstone walls that Pastor Johanna had strengthened in the dry season.

The Pastor was weeding between the lines of maize but he stopped and greeted us warmly.

'Can I help?' asked Adrian and picked up a spare hoe.

Johanna laughed. 'If you wish,' he said.

Melinda pointed to the water then sat on the ground and started taking off her shoes.

'Do you want to paddle?' laughed Rebecca then turned to me. 'It's quite safe.'

She kicked off her sandals, took Margaret from her back and dangled her toes in the water which made the child squeal in delight.

I followed suit and held Melinda's hand then we both cooled our feet in the shallows. As I looked down I noticed some small fish darting away from us.

Melinda pulled my hand so she could get a closer look.

'What are they?' I asked Rebecca.

'They are called tilapia. My brothers like to catch them for my mother to cook.' She looked up at the sky. 'But

150

sometimes the fish eagle comes to eat them.'

'Do they taste good?'

'They are very good. My father says he has heard that you can breed them to sell, maybe he will do that sometime.'

'I'm afraid there won't be any for supper tonight,' I said as Melinda splashed her feet in the water and the fish swam away.

'You must come back here with Melinda when she is older so she can see where she and Margaret used to play.'

The sun went behind a cloud and for a moment the valley was cast in shadow.

'That would be lovely,' I said, 'and, whatever happens I'll always remember this place.'

I stood in silence soaking up the atmosphere until Adrian and Johanna emerged carrying cobs of sweet corn and some guavas.

'Hajara will cook the corn for us to share and the guavas are very sweet to eat,' said Johanna as he led the way back to his compound.

A large kettle was boiling on the fire and Rebecca's mother poured tea for us then put the corn on a griddle to roast. When we were all sitting down I gave Hajara a jar of marmalade made from oranges I had bought in the market. Then Melinda gave Margaret the basket of clothes and toys.

Rebecca was delighted and jumped up. I have a gift for you too,' she said and went to her sleeping hut. A moment later she handed me a pillow case with the words 'Sleep Well Dear.' carefully embroidered in the centre.

'It's beautiful, did you make it yourself?' I felt very touched.

'Of course! I made it so you will sleep well when you are far away from here.'

'Thank you. I will treasure it.'

It was almost dark as we walked back to the car but Venus was shining brightly in the east.

Our last day came all too quickly and packing kept being interrupted by a stream of visitors.

'I thought I'd come to the wrong house!' said Jim Wade as he peered through the open door.

'It does feel strange.' I looked at the bare walls as I tried to remember where we had packed everything.

'I wonder if you have room for one more memento to add to your collection,' Jim said diffidently.

I thought he was joking until I noticed he was holding something wrapped in a piece of cloth. He gave it to me just as Adrian came in from the garden.

'Jim has brought us something,' I said.

I unwrapped the gift and gasped when I lifted out a bronze chalice. It had intricate markings around the rim and the tiny pillar on which it stood. As I cupped it in my hands it felt just right, its coolness on my palms calming in the heat of the day.

I stammered my thanks and Adrian peered down to get a closer look then began to add his thanks but Jim was already leaving.

'It's a gift from the Mandara; cherish it well,' he said as he disappeared down the drive.

'I will,' I called.

And I still do.

# Chapter 22     Homecoming to a drought

'This is the Captain speaking. We are beginning our descent to Heathrow. The weather is sunny and the temperature is 86° Fahrenheit.'

I felt a mixture of excitement and trepidation as I looked down at the tightly packed rows of houses. Suddenly the streets gave way to parched earth surrounding the gravel pits and for a moment I felt I was back in Nigeria. I had braced myself for rain but it seemed our tropical experience was going to be extended as I caught a glimpse of goal posts and playground equipment marooned in patches of sun-baked grass.

Melinda hadn't slept well on the flight but, as soon as she saw Mum and Dad at the arrivals gate, she shouted and ran towards them. Once we had our luggage stowed in their Vanguard Estate Dad drove cautiously out of the airport. He pointed to a billboard displaying a notice banning the use of hosepipes and garden sprinklers.

'We heard about the situation on the World Service but hadn't realised it was so serious,' said Adrian.

Dad nodded. 'Parliament has just passed a Drought Act. But we'll manage. I've started using bath water on my tomatoes.'

Unlike much of the population we all revelled in the heat that summer. Mum and Dad liked nothing better than relaxing in the garden when they came home from work. We had feared that the temporary addition of a toddler to their household would cause problems but the weather enabled Melinda to have the freedom to play outside all day.

Mum organised a family reunion in the garden and I enjoyed catching up with my aunts and cousins as well as my brother. We also felt free to invite our friends without encroaching on Mum and Dad's privacy inside the house.

Jill and Dave had returned a couple of months before us and bought a house in Oxfordshire where Dave was about to take up a post as a science teacher. Melinda and Jemima were delighted to see each other again and we were able to share our experiences, both of Nigeria, and the equally challenging task of acclimatising to life Back Home.

***

A lot of the summer was spent house hunting in Lincolnshire where Adrian would be working. We took our tiny caravan to a wooded holiday park on the Wolds. It was a relaxing place to return to each evening after looking round a variety of houses and finding it almost impossible to imagine what they would be like in winter. The process was complicated because Adrian's parents, Helen and Ernest, decided they wanted to live near us so we were negotiating two sets of house purchases.

When we received notification that our air freight had arrived we returned to Surrey, hired a van and collected it from Heathrow. We stacked our cargo in Mum and Dad's back yard and, with no rain on the horizon, it remained there until we moved.

'Are you going to open them to check everything's arrived safely?' Mum asked looking longingly at the boxes with their airline stickers.

'I can't believe we bought so much stuff!' I said as we opened the first box.

Apart from one of the pottery finials, everything had survived the journey intact. We had calabashes, pottery god pots and drinking vessels, bead necklaces, plaited grass mats, java print cloth, an ebony carving and several bronze items including the chalice.

Most items had a story to tell and it was several hours before we wrapped them back up carefully and stored them away in their boxes.

***

The drought lasted long enough for us to establish

ourselves in our cottage in a village on the edge of the Lincolnshire Wolds. It ended dramatically at the beginning of term with rain sweeping across the country throughout September. This wasn't an easy time for us or for Adrian's parents who were living in our caravan at the bottom of our garden until their own house in a neighbouring village was ready.

When they moved out we were able to establish some sort of routine although Melinda was puzzled by the constraints of her new life and kicked off her shoes whenever she could. Once again I experienced pangs of homesickness but this time it was for the wide African skies, the sharp scent of Harmattan and the sound of cicadas, cowbells and the distant beat of drums.

Two years later, with Melinda and her little sister Emily, we packed our bags again and flew south for our new life on the edge of the Kalahari.

# Chapter 23    Dejas Vue in Los Molinos

I woke up with a feeling of anticipation. Melinda had been away seven weeks and I was looking forward to hearing about her time in Andalusia. She was about to start her third year of an Environmental and Development Studies degree and had just returned from a project in southern Spain.

The rest of the family were still asleep as I walked past our calabashes on the landing wall and went downstairs. In the hallway was a carved chest that used to be Melinda's toy box and now held our slides from Nigeria, Botswana and Ghana.

It was already warm outside and I took my tea into the garden where I was welcomed by bleating from our sheep hoping for a titbit. I picked up a couple of early windfalls and threw them over the field gate. There was a squawking from the chicken shed and I made a mental note to collect the eggs later.

'Hi Mum!'

Melinda was striding towards me, her face bronzed by the sun and her hair several shades lighter.

'You're up early!'

'I'm used to it. They work you hard at Sunseed!' She looked at the cloudless sky. 'I can't believe it's so warm!'

'And I can't believe how the time flies. It's the hottest summer since the 1976 drought and that was nineteen years ago!'

There was a quacking from the orchard and four ducks waddled in a line to a plastic paddling pool under the hazelnut tree. One of the drakes flapped its wings as it landed in the pool with a splash while the other ducks foraged for delicacies.

'There were more ducks when I left.' Melinda looked at me questioningly.

'The fox came soon afterwards.' I shrugged and changed the subject. 'I expect you'd like some breakfast.'

'That sounds good, I'm starving!'

I noticed that Melinda had lost weight. 'What was the food like?'

'It depended who was cooking. Everything was vegetarian and we grew loads of vegetables. We took it in turns to cook but some of the volunteers didn't know how to! The nearest shop is over an hour's walk away. And we certainly didn't have our milk delivered!' she added as we heard a clink of bottles and Mr Bates, the milkman, walked up the drive.

'I want to hear all about it but we'll wait until everyone's up,' I said as we went back into the house.

'How are the French students?' Melinda asked as she tucked into her breakfast.

'They're a nice lot this year and the teachers are good and so is the French leader. Emily's doing well as an assistant, she says she might like to teach the students next summer. And Alyrene's enjoying bringing a friend on the trips; it's Flamingo Land next week.'

'Have you anyone coming in September?'

When we returned from Botswana I had started Wold School of English, running language courses from our home, mainly for Europeans preparing to work on development projects overseas. I also hired classrooms at the local secondary school and ran summer schools for French teenagers whose parents worked for the bank, Credit Lyonnaise, which organised holidays for the children of their staff.

'AGEH, the German development organisation, are sending a physiotherapist who is preparing to work with disabled children in Zambia.'

We were interrupted by the phone ringing.

'I hope that's not one of the host families with a problem,' I said as I hurried into my tiny office to answer it.

Fortunately there were no problems to deal with that day and I was able to relax in the garden and listen to Melinda's traveller's tales. Emily and Alyrene bombarded her with questions about the people and social life which seemed to revolve almost entirely around the volunteers at Sunseed.

After she had satisfied their curiosity Melinda announced, 'I'm going back! And you must visit me.'

'There's so much I want to show you,' she continued. 'We're using permaculture techniques for sustainable agriculture and we're fixing the irrigation tunnels built by the Moors. There's an earth dam across the river and a lovely fresh water pool; it's so peaceful and I know you'll love it!'

'Sounds as if we've got next year's holiday sorted!' said Adrian looking pleased.

***

A year later we waved Melinda goodbye as she and two friends set off for Spain in her little 2CV. In the October half term we flew with Alyrene to spend a week with friends who, by happy coincidence, had a house only a half hour drive from the project where Melinda worked.

Melinda met us at the airport and drove us to our friends in the picturesque village of Bédar.

The next day Melinda took us to Sunseed.

'We're nearly there,' she said and pulled into a layby. 'You get a good view from here.'

The hot dry air fleetingly reminded me of Nigeria as I looked at the river snaking through the deep valley below.

'And that's Sunseed down there!' Melinda pointed down the rocky hillside.

We got back in the car and soon turned off the main road.

'It's a good thing your car's a 2CV,' said Adrian as we bumped over a rock on the rough track, 'Most other vehicles would be complaining by now.'

We parked near a white washed building with blue paintwork and Melinda introduced us to some of the other volunteers. Someone brought a pot of tea, mugs and a tin of powdered milk which we drank under a canopy of grape vines secured by wooden posts.

'Now I'll show you round!' said Melinda when we had finished our tea. 'I'll give you a proper tour later but first I want to show you the dam I was telling you about.'

She led us past the vegetable beds, through the olive grove and down a steep slope to the river.

It was almost midday and there was a gentle hum of insects as the sun beat down on us. Ahead was a pool big enough to swim in and at one end was the dam that had been carefully made by unknown hands. As we stood there I felt a sense of peace that was rooted in distant memory.

'I just love this place. I almost feel I've been here before.' Melinda said.

Adrian and I looked at each other in amazed silence.

Finally I said, 'It's extraordinary. This feels just like Pastor Johanna's Dam in Nigeria. We used to take you there and it was a place where we always felt relaxed and happy.'

'But I couldn't remember it, could I? I was only a baby when we left Nigeria.'

'You were twenty months old. I think happy memories remain with us to be cherished.'

'That's a lovely thought. But how will I remember the other things that happened when I was growing up in Nigeria?'

I laughed. 'Maybe I'll write a book about it sometime!'

## Gude participants in the survey

| CONTRIBUTERS | RESIDENCE | RELIGION | OCCUPATION |
|---|---|---|---|
| **Rebecca Sylvester** | Sahuda | Christian | **Student** at Mubi TTC |
| Pastor Johanna & Hajara | Sahuda | Christian | Pastor/Farmer |
| Mary | Sahuda | Christian | Farmer |
| Usman and wives | Sahuda | Muslim | Farmer |
| Aliyu and wives | Sahuda | Muslim | Farmer |
| **Hannatu Dadi** | Njairi | Christian | **Student** at Mubi Sec School |
| Mary Dadi | Njairi | Christian | Local midwife |
| Jacob Dadi | Njairi | Christian | Farmer/Blacksmith |
| Ester | Njairi | Christian | Soldier's wife |
| Aishatu | Njairi | Pagan | Farmer |
| Lami,Maimuna, Fadi, Lami | Njairi | Muslim | Wealthy trader's wives |
| **Hajara Audu** | Mubi | Muslim | **Student** at Mubi Sec School |
| Sadaatu Audu | Mubi | Muslim | Cook at primary school |
| Amina Mahmudu | Mubi | Muslim | Farm Centre Principal's wife |
| Mr Dauda | Mubi | Muslim | Local government officer |
| Hiatu's mother[1] | Mubi | Muslim | Trader/Blacksmith - son |
| **Ahmed** | Mubi | Muslim | **Student** at Mubi TTC |
| **Marcus** | Lamurde | Muslim | **Student** at Mubi TTC |
| Chief Ardo | Lamurde | Pagan | Farmer/Herbalist |
| Awo Mado | Lamurde | Pagan | Witchdoctor/Blacksmith |
| Marcus's father[2] | Lamurde | Pagan | Farmer/Blacksmith |

160

| | | | |
|---|---|---|---|
| Marcus's mother | Lamurde | Pagan | Potter |
| Pastor Ibrahim & wife | Lamurde | Christian | Pastor/Farmer |
| Pastor Bullus & Sorya | Lamurde | Christian | Pastor/Farmer |
| Mariama Musa | Lamurde | Christian | Farmer/Carpenter – husband |
| Hatki Kininga | Lamurde | Pagan | Farmer/Blacksmith – husband |
| Ladi Saidu | Lamurde | Pagan | Farmer |
| Kiyi | Lamurde | Pagan | Farmer |
| Maksha | Lamurde | Christian | Farmer/Blacksmith – husband |
| Kuji[3] | Lamurde | Pagan | Farmer |
| Mallam Yaro[4] | Lamurde | Muslim | Healer – Quranic medicine |
| Chief Aliyu | Girimburum | Pagan | Farmer |
| Rugwa | Girimburum | Pagan | Farmer |
| Chief Dompwa[5] | Gella | Pagan | Farmer |

*1. **Haiatu** is a blacksmith originally from Gella. He began trading in brass three years earlier. His mother lives in his compound and recently became a Muslim.*

*2. **Marcus's parents** were Pagan when I first met them.*

*3. **Kuji** is an intermediary between people and the gods. When people are in trouble she tells them which god to offer sacrifice to.*

*4. **Mallam Yaro** was the first man from Lamurde to move from the top of the mountain when he became a Muslim but he was determined to remember the Pagan traditions. He told us about the genealogy of the clan in Lamurde.*

*5. **Chief Dompwa** is from the same clan as the Lamurde chief. His compound had burnt down and was being re-built when we visited.*

# Letter from Marcus

*31st August 1976 Marcus S Ahmed Lamorde*
*Mubi TTC*
*Gongola State*

*Dear Mr and Mrs Rosser*

*I am very glad to have the full opportunity of writing these few lines in order to know more about your present condition of health.*

*On my own personal affairs I am very well. Don't take this letter as a surprise because I didn't write to you since.*

*How was the journey from Mubi to your area? I hope you have made successfully and enjoyably. How did you meet your parents. I hope they are all in good condition? My parents are extending their greetings to all of you and more especially Melinda.*

*Please Sir, if possible I want some copy to send for me because there are some people who said they want to see it more especially the one I took at Gwoza during my visit to my friend Buba Shelm. I sent the first film on the 12th of July 76 maybe it will reach you safely although this is my first time of taking photo.*

*Comments on the first film. 1, 2, 3 and 4 had been taken during the marriage ceremony of Ardo's daughter Nuda. 10, 11 and 12 are some gods which our forefathers were worshipping. 10 is a god known as Chingum, 11 is a god known as grenna, 12 is a god known as vieva. All in Lamorde.*

*The rest of the film is of vegetation.*

*Comments on the second film. In film 1 you will find a corn known as jigari ready for harvest and also groundnuts plant which is still young. 3 and 4 were taken at Bahuli when I went for visit during the vacation. 5 – Ardo during blacksmithing. 6 woman getting ready for market. 7 & 8 Group of women and men during community work on the far. 9 – 20 were taken at Gwoza*

162

*during visit to my friend Buba Musa Shehu. In the last film*
*you will find Lauan and his child and group of women and*
*some buthers selling meat just on the ground. That is all.*
*So Sir kindly enough to serve me from Gwoza people.*
*Thanks be to God.*

*Yours. Marcus S. Ahmed. Lamorde.*

Sadly, I did not receive the first film. I thanked Marcus for his letter but did not receive a reply. Unless his family paid for a mail box at the Post Office, the only way Macus could receive mail when he left the TTC was in his place of employment.

# Letter from Rebecca

*19th January 1977 Vimtim Primary School*
*Mubi L.E.A*
*Gongola State*
*Nigeria*

*Dear Mrs Rosser*

*It's me Rebecca saying hello to you this night. I am greeting you in the name of our lord Jesus Christ. How are you, your husband and your parents and my little Melinda, I hope they are all well.*

*My aim of writing you this letter to you is to let you know that I have got your letter and to inform you about my sorrow.*

*Oh my dear sister it will be a shock to you that my dear Daddy is dead, he was killed in a motor accident. A lorry knocked him down between Sahuda and Bokoula. He died on the 13th of November on Saturday around 9.00 am in 1976. He left my Mummy under state but now she has delivered a baby girl by name Lawi.*

*Our grade two result is also out and I missed one paper that is Maths, I had 6 pass and 2 merits in Literature and Religion but all the rest are ordinary pass.*

*Please send my greetings to all known faces.*

*Yours*

*Mrs Rebecca Sylvester*

*PS I am expecting another baby in August 1977*

I was shocked and upset by Rebecca's letter and wrote to her straight away. However, I did not receive a reply.

# Ray Williams' Diary

Many of the details mentioned in this memoir would not have been possible without reference to the diary my father wrote during his short stay in the Mandara. His sense of humour combined with a meticulous eye for detail make for a very enjoyable read. The original diary is over 12,000 words but I have edited it for punctuation and taken out some repetition and superfluous information.

## Ray Williams' Nigerian Diary

### 13th December 1973 – 11th January 1974

### Thursday 13th December

Boarded British Caledonian flight No. 355. Boeing 707. Take off 10.15 p.m.

Height 33,000 — 39,000 feet. Dinner served approx. 11.00 p.m.

### Friday 14th December

Landed Kano airport 4.45 a.m. Very warm night - no moon. Heather & Adrian there to meet us. Cleared customs and off to Central Hotel.

Visited Kano market in the old city. Hired a guide to take us through the maze of alleys. Adrian bought a tie dye cotton tablecloth and carved walking stick after tough bargaining.

Returned to hotel for bath and siesta. Watched kites and vultures soaring over Kano then evening meal and early to bed.

### Saturday 15th December

Motored around Kano. There were vast numbers of bicycles, goats, hand carts, lorries, beggars. Traffic drives on the horn so it's one continual hubbub. Saw Emir's Palace – very Eastern and impressive.

Shopped in area around hotel. Bought small thorn carving of a pair of draught players, one skin bag, and a flat unnamed musical instrument made from guinea corn stalks. Later bought two lumps of blue agate for 1 naira each.

After dinner had drinks in hotel courtyard under a warm tropical star studded sky watching the large fruit bats flitter around the illuminated neem trees.

### Sunday 16th December

Set off for Lake Baguda 36 miles south of Kano on the Zaria road. The lake has recently been formed by the construction of the Tiga Dam across the Hadejia River. After approx. one hour we arrived at the Lake Baguda hotel complex. This has only been opened a few months and was on a 130 acre site facing the dam's lake. It was a single story design consisting of a large dining room, bar and conference area. Accommodation was provided by 108 chalets and 4 suites. We paid 18.90 naira per night for our 4 person hut including breakfast for 4 which was only about £5 each b & b. The cuisine was excellent, the hotel was practically empty and at times we had the Olympic sized swimming pool completely to ourselves.

By the lakeside was a large tree surrounded with a comfortable circular seat where we watched an abundance of birds and insects. There were three types of dragon-fly. One had transparent gossamer wings with a broad chocolate brown banding and delicate yellow gold peripheral line picking out the wing profile. At rest it settled with nose to wind.

Swam p.m. Wonderful evening dinner. Finished evening outside our hut star gazing against the background of an intense indigo sky, swatting mosquitoes and sipping Champagne Brandy.

## Monday 17th. December.

A day around the hotel. Noted many small conical depressions in sandy path approx. ¾"dia x 1" deep. These were the prey traps of the ant lion. Cut off top of small harvester termite mound and noted stored grain and grass inside.

Motored along small road near hotel, saw camel train coming south from desert. Tried to photograph but frustrated by villagers demanding money. Returned to lake and watched many birds. Hazel disturbed small black snake. More swimming and fine meals.

## Tuesday 18<sup>th</sup> December

Checked out of hotel early after leaving a parting gift of bananas to resident pata monkeys outside reception office.

### Lake Bagauda to Zaria - 75 miles Direction South West.

New wild life: grey hornbill and eagles (unidentified).

Crops: guinea corn, cotton, eucalyptus and red peppers. The red peppers were being harvested and put onto the mud roofs of houses for drying which added vivid patches of colour to a baked countryside.

Many long horned, humped back, brown and white cattle. Many villages near roadside which were often completely surrounded by a reddish-brown mud wall approx. 7 ft. high. The huts were mud rather than grass. In some of the more prosperous villages there were most attractive murals on the outer walls. Many of the trees were buttressed round the trunk as the roots are shallow and this increases their wind resistance.

### Zaria to Joss - 150 miles- direction south east.

Zaria was a typical African shanty town with an enormous

modern post office set back in its own grounds. Stopped for petrol and besieged by traders and beggars. Bought a large bunch of very green looking local bananas, apparently all bananas in Africa are green but the fruit is nicely ripe.

Turned left off main Kaduna road in centre of town and drove south-east along a B road. Soon after leaving the town, the road became a metalled narrow single track road flanked on each side with hard packed red laterite verges. Each verge was wide enough for a vehicle to overtake. It also enabled terrified cyclists to flee from the roaring, horn blowing motor traffic, which can be quite a frightening experience when encumbered by flowing robes, a sack of corn balanced on the head and with only a few months' experience of a recent change to driving on the right.

Herds of cattle were much larger and all white. Farming was mainly cotton, sugar cane and tobacco. A fish farm was also noted. The villages became more numerous but the buildings more primitive - all grass huts with grass compound walls. Road rising steadily upwards towards the vast Joss plateau for about 40 miles. Then the metalling on the road ran out altogether and became a wide red rocky track for between 30 and 40 miles, when it ran through a wild rocky area of a mixture of rolling mountains of black granite dotted with scrub and small trees. After coming over the edge of the plateau many small farms had high cactus hedges surrounding the huts and small fields to stave off the ravages of goats. We joined an A road about 50 miles from Joss and many stretches were wide and well metalled. Along the side of the road we noticed small swirling tornadoes of sand known locally as sand devils. As we dropped down into Joss, which is in a slight basin in the midst of the huge Joss plateau, the scenery changed and looked like an intensely hot Yorkshire moorland scene.

Arrived at Joss about 4.30 p.m. to claim our reservations at the Rest House but they had been lost. Finally got settled into the Herwa Motel, an ultra-modern

4 maisonette block. Our suite consisted of a large lounge off which were two double bedrooms with private bath and toilet to each room, a third W.C., a fully equipped kitchen with fridge and a steward. All for the equivalent of about £12 per night including breakfast i.e. £3 per head. Apparently General Gowan's brother stayed at our particular suite the week before. It also turned out that our steward had a son training to be a teacher at T.T.C. Mubi.

While we were settling in a trader came from an area well known for its thorn carvings. Bought carved chess set for Adrian's Christmas present, a delicate Nativity set and about a dozen exquisite village figures for about £6.10 which was about 2 shillings each. I looked at the man's hands which were cut in many places and it turned out that he was indeed a carver and not just a trader.

Had evening meal at the rest house and early to bed.

### Wednesday 19thDecember

Adrian put car in for 12,000 mile service and persuaded the garage into lending him the works car free of charge.

We visited the museum while Heather & Adrian went off on a major shopping expedition to replenish their cold store and stocks of European food. There was a large display of Nigerian tribal pottery all made without the potter's wheel. There were also several old vintage shunting engines on show and a magnificent steam traction engine.

After they met us we climbed Gowan's hill at side of museum but the view from top did not compensate for the exhausting climb.

We saw lemons growing outside zoo and hundreds of fruit bats hanging high up in the tall neem and mahogany trees. Went round the zoo which was very pleasant and informal.

Had lemonade and cakes in a replica of a Benin Palace. It was in fact a very large single storeyed house, with a thick grass roof. Sticking out of the roof were many carved wooden figures. In the centre of the house was a sunken courtyard open to the sky. The mud walls were smooth and coloured with red ochre.

Went round two book shops after lunch. Cashed £100 travellers' cheques at 6.35 Naira to the £1 which was a very poor exchange rate. Watched Heather & Adrian haggle for vegetables and pick out potatoes one by one. Adrian bought Heather a delicate silver filigree bracelet and I for Hazel a fur covered handbag - both Christmas presents. Then followed a sterling/naira transaction where for £50 notes obtained 900 to the £1. (approx. 15% above the morning rate).

Took Heather & Adrian to the Hill Station hotel for evening meal. Bought Hazel a small necklace and Adrian bought an African talking drum from a trader outside the hotel. Met the English family who shared Lake Baguda with us (The Coopers) - he worked for the British Council. In 1961 it took him 4 days and 400 gallons of petrol to get from Joss to Mubi on the bush roads as they then existed. Hoped for better things tomorrow!!

## Thursday 20th December

**Joss to 20 Mubi - 380 miles.**

Owing to the great heat of around 120-130°F the driving technique is to close all the car windows to keep out the fine red dust and to prevent the hot wind from literally skinning one. Driver and passengers sit on thick towels to soak up the sweat. Adrian had fitted an electric fan on the shelf behind the rear seat which prevented the concentration of heat due to solar radiation through the windows.

The first leg of the journey was to Bauchi approx. 80 miles. We first climbed onto the summit of the plateau. The country was mountainous with large areas of forest reserve. Near Bauchi we left the main road and took our, by now perilously overloaded car, 8 kilometres up an atrocious bush track to the small village of Genji. Here on an outcrop of rock we saw some ancient rock drawings. Some of the men wore goatskin round their middle. They were offering for sale models of bicycles and lorries made from guinea corn pith, but they were too fragile to buy. Two men watched us inspecting the rock drawings, one had a bicycle that he kept dusting every few minutes. The other suffered from an eye infection that caused the lids to droop and eventually leads to blindness. We gave one of them our empty squash bottle which he received as if it were a bar of gold. This area was dotted with many silver coloured cactus-like bushes, which when a branch was fractured, exuded a thick milk-like fluid which is used locally as an effective gum.

We regained the main road, having to evacuate the car twice to enable Adrian to negotiate particularly deep pot holes. The 10 hour journey was interspersed by small townships: Gombe, Bui, Little Gombe and Hong. Along the banks of the dried up bed of the Gongola river between Gombe and Biu were many shea nut palms, which to the uninitiated look like coconut palms.

Arrived Mubi in near darkness, drove through the narrow main street flanked by people, pigs and goats. Adrian put foot on accelerator and hand on horn. We arrived at their house about a mile out of town - safe and tired. Big welcome from Usman in the form of a low sweeping bow with the back of the right hand touching the floor. In Islamic culture parents are revered so parents of Master and Madam get the full "Ranke Dede." Evening meal all prepared - house absolutely charming.

### Friday 21st & Saturday 22nd December

Met many of Heather's colleagues who live on the TTC compound or the G.R.A. (Government Residential Area). Had a brief look round the science labs of the T.T.C. and introduced to the Principal. The college was built in 1950 and is surrounded by groves of mahogany, guava (a sort of

171

apple), grape-fruit, lemon and palm-nut trees. These give welcome shade to the classrooms. Temperature in house 92°F.

Went to Mubi market. Hazel bought a highly coloured prayer mat for Nigel and received a small gift of Nigerian perfume from the trader. Noted that blacksmiths in the market kept well apart from the other traders.

Put up Christmas decorations. Visited Helen and Keith for supper.

Descended on by friends from Maiduguri - Lyall Watts, his wife Marge and Lyall's drunken cousin on holiday from Canada. A somewhat hilarious evening with all sorts of people milling around. Marge and the children slept in Richard's house nearby, Lyall and his cousin slept in their Estate car.

## Sunday 23rd December

Sunday, being Ahmadu's day off, I volunteered to water garden - hard at it until 1 p.m. - most exhausting.

Adrian had flat tyre and took spare to Mubi for repair.

Adrian killed and dressed pig. John Button (Principal of Secondary School) volunteered his steward to wash it afterwards, which he did with OMO. Adrian very tired after the butchering.

Had siesta then set out about 4 p.m. to Sahuda 14 miles along a bush road, saw pata monkeys. Crossed Nigerian frontier post and parked in "no-mans-land" between Nigerian and Cameroon borders. Fantastic view over rolling hills. Met one of the Mubi market traders.

Returned to Mubi for spare wheel (now dark). Garage owner had gone home and taken wheel with him for safe keeping. Took a guide aboard and drove through the dark narrow twisting mud-wall lined streets of the town. No lighting. Huddled be-robed figures sat outside their houses squatting around a communal food bowl. A few houses were lit by small paraffin hurricane lamps. Collected the spare and paid 6/ equivalent. Went to Helen and Keith for supper and met Peter the young Canadian volunteer.

## Monday 24th December

Early morning walk. In afternoon went to Mararaba, about 10 miles from Mubi on the Maiduguri road, to collect eggs from the Kulp Bible School mission. This is run partly by Dick and Kitty Winfield. Dick is an ordained American Pastor. In their garden saw tangerines and locus beans growing. We were invited to a meal after Christmas which we accepted with pleasure.

## Tuesday 25th December

In place of breakfast, very fine Brandy-laced egg nog which accompanied grand present opening. Would you believe it, the fine twisted walking stick purchased at Kano market and the talking African drum bought in Jos were for me. Hazel had a great surprise in receiving a fine green gown made from Nigerian printed cotton. Heather and Adrian were delighted with their meat slicer. Before lunch there were many visitors, including their best friends, Keith and Helen, who gave us a wonderful carved mask, and VSO teachers Anne and Ian.

As Usman and Ahmadu are Muslims they were on duty over the holiday, their turn came with the Muslim festival of Salah in January. This was fortunate as Christmas lunch in the heat of the African sun consisted of: turkey with sago stuffing, beef sausage, peas, carrots, green beans, bread sauce, boiled and roast potatoes, followed by Christmas pudding, sauce and mince pies, and the washing up of that lot would have been terrible. In all a very wonderful day but very hard on the stomach.

## Wednesday 26th December

Although Mubi market is open 7 days a week, each Wednesday is Market Day, when villagers and traders come from miles around to buy and sell. The differing colours and styles of dress both male and female were as diverse as the goods offered for sale. There was a wide range of vegetables and fruit such as peppers, spinach, tomatoes, mangoes. There were all types of pottery cooking pot (village made) and whole stalls with brightly enamelled Chinese bowls. Hazel bought a pair of bright red and white enamel casserole dishes.

Raw cotton, hand spun cotton, hand-woven 4" wide strips of cotton, and widths of cotton cloth made by machining together the 4" strips were persistently offered - "Welcome Madam - very-good-price Madam."

Some of the other stalls had the weirdest selection of what were doubtless the ingredients for local "witch-medicines" or even "ward-off" tokens. These included: porcupine quills, a crocodile's snout, a pair of revolting looking dried-up skeletal hornbills, a dried crow, bits of assorted animal skins, seed pods, medicinal wood and several types of bark. Also on the same stall were "do-it-yourself" medicine kits wrapped in dirty-looking coloured cloth. Having, however, made these disparaging remarks concerning local medicine, it is noteworthy that if any of the students of the T.T.C. are smitten with jaundice they are given formal official leave for treatment in their home village by local medicine.

At one stall there were some small nuggets of antimony ore which resembled anthracite nuts but it was crystalline and reflective. This is bought locally, ground up, and used as eye shadow.

Adrian bought for us to take home to his mother, a native ladies "modesty cover". This consisted of an 8" x 4" rectangle of "cloth" constructed from George V African 1/10th penny pieces. One of the short sides was ornamented with very small conch shells.

One striking figure in the market was one of the Lamido's bodyguards. This very tall man was dressed in a fine red loose fitting robe with a matching turban-like headdress. The Lamido these days occupies an office similar to that of Mayor except that the office is traditional and hereditary, he has little legal power but great influence.

Bought two pairs of calabashes for Nigel as ordered - cost 7/- the lot. These are actually scooped out gourds - the fruit of the bottle gourd tree. Hazel bought some cloth for curtains.

There were some Fulani women in the market, they were extremely beautiful in their wrap-round green cotton traditional style dress and finely plaited hair. Adrian bought some dark brown lumpy semi-liquid concoction which turned out to be wild honey which was superb. Five large ladles cost 5/- and was about 1-2lb.

A great deal of the merchandise is brought in panniers born by miniscule donkeys nearly off white in colour. The panniers are made from cow hide, they are very thick and hand sewn with thin strips of hide. Evidence of traders from the Cameroon Republic was apparent from a smattering of French here and there and the money-changers sitting cross-legged behind their piles of notes.

Whilst I write this, a tall man with a bundle on his head and wearing a fine red flowing gown, has just taken a short cut right through the middle of the garden.

Light lunch followed by siesta in preparation for the Principal's party. Saw the new-moon. In this latitude it is an upside down crescent with the tips pointing upwards. The air is so clear that one can see the complete outline of the rest of the moon with the naked eye. The party a great success, mainly in the garden surrounded by coloured lights hung from the frangipani trees. Excellent cold buffet, games and dancing, home at 2.a.m.

### Thursday 27th December

Bird watching with John Button, Principal of Government Secondary School. He took us in his Land Rover to a valley in Mandara Mountains. Followed bush path, over two water splashes and two villages surrounded by cactus scrub. Both were "leaf-lady" villages but the men wore trousers and cotton singlets. The bird watching valley was cultivated and a bit boggy. Guinea corn and rice were under cultivation. In 1½ hours we identified 23 species that I had not seen before.

It was dark on the return home and there was not a single light coming from any of the huts of either village. There was one small camp fire with a few figures huddled over it. We picked up several nightjars in the headlights and their eyes glittered like red cats-eyes. There had been a very slight Harmattan all day but not enough to dull the sun, only sufficient to blur the sharpness of the distant hills.

### Friday 28<sup>th</sup> December

An even more fabulous day than any we had yet experienced. A slightly later start than we had anticipated owing to the main "Gaz" cylinder running out, which we had to replace immediately as the fridge runs off gas. We set off for an all day trip to Rhumsiki. It is in the Cameroon Republic about 40/50 very rough miles from Mubi through the Mandara Mountains and lies approx. 30 miles beyond the Nigerian border.

The use of dry stone walling in the villages was immediately apparent. Great piles of grey and black granite formed small hills breaking up the landscape. Also upthrusting from the "moorland" were conical dry grass-covered hills rising some 200/300 ft. Some were studded with stunted trees giving, on silhouette, the impression of sparsely spined hedgehogs.

As we proceeded towards Rhumsiki the natural rock sculpture became more fantastic, with rocks surmounting rocks in seemingly impossible positions of balance. The small village of Rhumsiki was between 5000/6000 ft. and lay at the head of an enormous half gorge, half valley into which the adjoining mountains plunged, snaked and dropped sheer in alternating audacity until lost in the distant haze of a light harmattan. From where we stood, the entrance to the valley was guarded by a staggering 500 ft. monolith of granite burnished smooth by eons of elemental erosion that had bared vertical striations of pink, grey and brown. It stood serene and silent, as a warning to those who would explore further the boundless realms it guarded.

Lunch was partaken at an unobtrusively designed French restaurant, built in African style, but offering a truly French cuisine. Crudités, cauliflower cheese, roast guinea fowl with buttered turnips, finishing with fingers of plain short pastry dipped in apple purée. Coffee on the terrace was in company with "La Pic de Rhusiki" the French name for the great rock.

We continued for a few miles and every now and then were beset by small black French-speaking boys out to beg, or otherwise extort "dash", (money), bic pens or sell some item of brass or other bric-a-brac. We bought for the sum of 12/6 a small stringed instrument reputed to be called a Zimal.

The road wound gently upwards and we spotted four pata monkeys and a couple of mongooses. We turned back at a village where there were two more bizarre rock formations known as "Finger Mountain."

### Saturday 29th December

Went to market a.m. Hazel bought dress length for Sandra. Heather bought some cloth for Christine. Hazel collected some curtains she was having made-up in the market. Most markets seem to have a small battery of tailors sitting in the open, working away at their sewing machines. Some of them do very intricate embroidery, it is an all male craft.

After lunch Adrian and I potted a scorpion in clear polyester casting resin. Played chess with Adrian using thorn carved pieces, made a couple of careless moves and lost.

Went to Anne and Ian's to photograph a chameleon that

had taken up residence in their garden, 9" long body, with similar length prehensile tail. Opened its mouth wide in anger when picked up by tail but its fierceness was negated by its toothlessness. I placed it on a black cardigan and watched it darken.

P.M. went to dinner with Kitty and Dick Winfield at Kulp Bible School. Nigerian food which had been cooked traditionally over three hot stones in a native cooking pot. The meal consisted of a kind of dumpling made from guinea corn called tue. The complete dish was called tuo-mei, the mei being a thick meaty soup spiced with hot red peppers. This was followed by pork and potatoes with stick beans garnished with chopped onions. Played "Yatsee" and lost. As the mission electricity generator was turned off at 10 p.m. we carried on by the light of a paraffin lamp reinforced by candles.

Before dinner we went round the mission farm with Dick who explained they were teaching crop rotation. This consists of first year guinea corn followed by cotton and ending with ground-nuts. Many bush people only crop guinea corn and move off the ground when it is exhausted, in which case, it takes about 10 years to regain its fertility if it has not been eroded before then. The basic course for qualifying as a Pastor is three years. The man comes with his wife and children, is given a hut, small garden and two acres of farmland. The land is split, 1 acre good land and the other somewhat poorer. This makes them self-supporting and after the course they will have accumulated a few luxuries such as a bicycle and clothing for the whole family. The wives as well as the man and his children are given education.

### Sunday 30th December

Harmattan seems to have left us completely. A 100 mile return picnic trip today to Michika and 12 miles into the bush beyond. We drove along the Maiduguri road. At first we lost the hills, but soon began to pass great rock jumbles. The road ran through many small villages including South Margi, about one hour's drive from the T.T.C and the furthest that Heather & Adrian have been for observing students on teaching practice. We passed through the small town of Baza, where goats and sheep on the road duly responded to the car's horn. Donkeys became immobile, usually broadside on to the car, whilst the pigs walked nose-to-ground across the road oblivious to all, the original "road hogs" no doubt.

We arrived at Michika, a small vibrant town, on market day. The colour and contrast of the women's dresses was gay, vivid and tasteful and surpassed the Mubi market day spectacle. The mixture of flamboyant tightly fitting wrap-round dresses and gay head-wraps blended naturally with the near no dress of Higgi women. We met some of Heather & Adrian's students and one of them escorted us round the market and bargained in Higgi for 3 earthenware bowls which she got for 3/—.

We left Michika and took a bush road towards Finger mountain. Stopped for a picnic at the currently unoccupied mission house at N'boro, having passed a resting place under a large tree where men were drinking burukatu. The road was steadily deteriorating into something approximating a wide stream bed. We passed a colourful wedding party, forded two small rivers and came to a group of old men with whom we talked to our mutual incomprehension but they did at least enjoy looking through my binoculars. We finally came to a wide mostly dried up river. It was the Nigerian Cameroon border, but the bank was so steep that we could get no further.

We met the old men again on the way back and drank burukatu with them. Burukatu is a beer served warm and made from guinea corn which is ground, mixed with water and boiled. It is left to stand for some days, more ground corn is added with possibly other additives such as pepper then it is re- boiled. It is filtered through what look like giant finger stalls made of plaited straw. They are about 18" long and between 4" to 6" in diameter. On our return between Baza and South Margi we passed a second wedding group, this time the ladies all wore identical dresses.

Went to Mubi Club p.m. and met the local deputy head of police, who was delighted to hear the story of Keith's friend who last week ran his car into a police station in the Cameroons, leaving his number plate firmly attached to the brickwork to prove it.

## Monday 31st December

After yesterday's marathon and in anticipation of tonight's New Year party, today was a pottering about-day. To Mubi market a.m. with Adrian to post letters, get groceries and buy loose salt. P.M. all of a flurry for the party, Hazel and Heather very active in the kitchen. Trader came to the door with an assortment of brass figures which we did not care for and some carved wooden figures. We bought a male and female figure for 6 naira the pair. I was "dashed" two small brass ornaments.

The New Year's Eve celebrations were a great success. We began with a wonderful meal to which Heather & Adrian had invited their three charming Italian friends. The main meal consisted of drunken duck (a good harbinger of what was to follow) sweet/sour rice etc. mince pies, fruit salad and ice cream (churned by R.W; at great sweat earlier). At about 9 p.m. the bachelors arrived (Richard, Chris, Emyr) plus Anne and Ian and Clive with his charming Nigerian wife Adelchi plus as ever Helen and Keith. The punch served from a large hollowed-out water melon was a great success and was re-filled and emptied several times. My recollections became somewhat blurred as the evening wore on but I do recall that the melon containing the punch got eaten prematurely by Anne.

Staggered to bed 1.30 a.m. wondering why Adrian and I had promised to meet John Button at 7.15 a.m. for bird watching.

# Tuesday 1st January

Met John Button approx. 7.15 a.m. Drove 9 miles on the Sahuda road to a small winding stream. Identified 36 new species in 4 exhausting hours. The most amazing bird behaviour observed was between two male green sandpipers at the stream edge. There was a savage fight in which legs were bitten and at one point the stronger of the two held his opponent's head under the water. The combat ended when the loser extricated himself and flew off.

Went for an evening walk along a rocky river bank. Came upon a rock on which bundles of benni seeds were drying. On the surface of the rock were many grinding depressions. Benni seeds are ground for their oil and used in cooking.

# Wednesday 2nd January

Up at the crack of dawn and left at 7.10 a.m. with Jauro, our guide who was one of the student teachers at the T.T.C. We were off to Sahuda to climb a steep hill that was in fact an ancient volcanic cone about 400 ft. high so far as one could judge. It was round at the base, rising steeply to the summit at an angle of about 45°. Small black boulders of heavy lava, presumably the remains of the last ancient eruption, lay tumbled down the north facing slope.

We set off over a reaped guinea corn field which due to the height, depth and width of the furrows, proved to be far more arduous than an English ploughed field. The first 2/3rds of the way up, though steep, was relatively easy. The dry standing grass was about 4 to 5 feet high and clouds of fine white pollen came off as we pushed our way through it. This gave Hazel hay fever for a day or two. The grass was intermingled with small springy scrub bushes which, fortunately, were seldom armed with the normally vicious long thorns so often encountered in these parts. The final leg of the ascent was stony and the going was most fatiguing. At the summit the rim was not as well formed as we had hoped.

The view, even by the superlatives of the Rhumsiki area, was staggering. To the south east stretched mountain range upon mountain range, a mixture of parched grass and black rock. A classical river valley zig-zagged towards the southwest into the distance. Its side, unblended by any glacial forces, fell sharply to the now dried-up river bed that would become a rushing torrent when the rains return in the spring. Looking south, as far as the eye could see there were scores of small farms, each surrounded by the cactus hedges so common in that area. To the north, the mountains swept away into further ranges and the lack of water was confirmed by the sight of only one small farm almost hidden by a few stunted trees. West and below us we could see the Nigerian frontier post and the small township of Sahuda. To the east, and with the aid of our field glasses, we could see the Cameroon customs post at Boukoula.

On the summit itself were the remains of a fortified encampment contained by four dry walls about 4 feet in height and made from black volcanic stones. Jauro explained that people of the Gude tribe lived on the summit during the early part of this century and that hills of this nature were often occupied as natural areas of defence and protection during the Fulani wars. When the hill was occupied the slopes were cultivated as far as possible and water was carried from the bottom on a relay system.

On the summit there were one or two thorn trees, many succulents and one of the brilliant red-flowering trees, around which darted two pygmy long tailed sunbirds, drawing nectar out of the blossoms with their long thin curved beaks. The downward trek was exhausting and took 5O mins - 10 mins. longer than the ascent.

Got back at noon and slept for two hours exhausted. To Mubi club pm. Met Ahmadu: medical secretary Mubi hospital, Bentunde: deputy provincial police officer and Joel: manager of Barclays bank Mubi. The last two did not stay long, but Ahmadu and I had a long talk and I was most impressed by his great courtesy in talking so long outside in the garden where I suspect he found it very cold indeed.

## Thursday 3rd January

Hazel and I woke up incredibly stiff from yesterday's climb and were pleased to have a quiet day. Usman was going home to his village for Salah and, as we will have started the long trek home by then, we gave him 5 naira in thanks for all the extra work our visit had made for him. We got a grand bow and fine smile. We think that this will assist him with his current financial negotiations with regard to his impending marriage.

P.M. as the ladies were getting a little tired of the constant male exodus on bird watching exercises, they accepted an invitation from the bachelors to go to Digal and watch Shadoof irrigation in action. They commented, somewhat darkly, on the courtesy with which they were treated and the pleasant nature of the expedition.

John Button took Adrian and I into the bush to visit the Chief of Bahuli in the Fali area. Unfortunately he was away at another village. A typical feature of chiefs' houses in this area is that they are often surmounted by an ostrich egg contained in an ornate clay "egg-cup". The opportunity for more bird watching was not to be missed which started with an unprecedented view of two pairs of ground hornbills who positively pranced around to enable us to view them from all angles in a most leisurely manner. More bird watching firsts on this occasion were a great white heron, a gabar goshawk, a hadada (Ibis family) and a bearded barbet.

Two of the old men sitting under the village tree were hand spinning cotton. One man was carding whilst the other was spinning. The speed with which the bobbin revolved, in response to the twisting of the fibres between finger and thumb, was incredible.

During our walk through the village we came across a small boy who had obviously never seen white people before and was bellowing with great terror, much to the amusement of his brothers and sisters. We returned in the dark, nearly got stuck in a dried-up river-bed, but John did eventually manage to engage four wheel drive and we climbed out.

After supper went over to Keith and Helen's and played Oil.

## Friday 4ᵗʰ January

Early start and in position at vantage point on rocks overlooking Mubi by 8.30 a.m. to witness the Muslim festival of Salah. The religious part of the festival is short and is followed by a display of horsemanship and ends in speeches by local dignitaries.

For the first hour we watched the Muslims assemble for the service. It was an all-male affair and fathers could be seen taking their small sons. The diversity of the colour of their dress was fantastic. They all wore loose flowing robes or caftans: whites, pale blues, yellow, orange, pale and vivid green with an occasional shiny black. Predominantly they wore hula hats, richly embroidered, but there was a thin scattering of very fine Arab type head-dress indicating that the wearer had made the great pilgrimage to Jedda (Mecca) and entitled him to the courtesy title Al-Hadji.

From time to time a horseman would wend his way across the dried-up river-bed. His horse would be richly bedecked and hung with brightly coloured woollen tassels of scarlet, blue and yellow. The saddle, saddle girth and saddle cloth was brightly adorned for the ceremonial occasion. The riders, whose attire was as flamboyant as that of their horses, bore either swords, or long copper-tipped spears. After all the faithful had assembled, I would estimate around two thousand, the call to prayer was heard.

The whole assembly bowed and touched the ground with their foreheads as demanded by Muslim custom and this mass movement from our vantage point resembled the gently waving of a huge coloured flag. At this point the obviously pagan Africans who were sitting near us burst into derisive laughter. After about ten minutes and several more acts of obeisance the service ended, the assembly dispersed and made its way to the town square flanked on one side by the Lamido's palace and on the other by the rear of the Mosque. Both these buildings were very modest affairs.

We got ourselves nicely settled on the shady side of the square where a couple of stone steps made useful seats. It took about 30 minutes before the crowd from the service started to drift in. The square was closed on three sides and open to the main approach road on the fourth. It was surfaced with fine white dusty sand.

The proceedings started by the appearance of a jester-cum-MC. He was dressed in an embroidered grey caftan and he wore a very long grey/green hat, similar to a chef's hat but longer and more slender. He sang and danced shaking a maraca. Then the band arrived consisting of a drummer supported by one horn and one trumpet player. The drums were various sizes but all were slung across the body and beaten with the tip of a curved thorn stick. The horn was something like an English hunting horn but double the length and more belled out. The trumpet was rudimentary. The Jester danced around singing and jesting, some of the time very obviously at our expense. At one point he removed his grey caftan to reveal underneath a bright orange one, which after more dancing, he stripped off to reveal a rich maroon one in which he finished his act.

The Lamido, robed in white, mounted on a richly ornamented horse and sheltered from the sun by an enormous multi-coloured sun-shade carried by one of his bodyguards, arrived escorted by a mounted escort of local chiefs. He took his place in the centre of the raised dais flanked by all the local V.I.Ps. Basically, the ceremony consisted in the mounted Chiefs galloping at full tilt to the dais and wheeling away. Initially they came three abreast but by the time the finale arrived, they came in at about twelve abreast. After the horsemanship there were long speeches in Hausa, the only words of which I understood were Federal Government. We dispersed quickly with the rest of the crowd for cold lunch and a well-earned siesta.

Late afternoon/evening a long cool walk towards the Digil area.

## Saturday 5<sup>th</sup> January

Left for picnic at about 11 a.m. Branched left off Maiduguri road along a wonderful bush road. Passed relatively few villages but the area had warning signs from the Ministry of Natural Resources indicating areas of cattle movement restriction due to bovine pleura- pneumonia. The disease is dangerous and can only be checked by a brutal slaughter policy as with foot and mouth in the U.K.

We drove through a lightly forested area and stopped at the bank of an almost dry river bed. We crossed on foot to enable Adrian to get a good run-up at the bank opposite which was a bit rough. We ran into farmed land as we were approaching a range of hills that ran east and west. At the small town of Pakka the road turned west. To the south, the high hills forming the Nigerian Cameroon border, to the north a large flat fertile plain with the Hong hills in the far distance. Dotted here and there were gigantic rock upthrusts so common a feature of this area. Pakka was a very small market town although it was not, unfortunately, market day. After leaving Pakka, the villages were few and far between. We continued for about 20 very rough miles which included fording three small rivers and finally arrived at the border town of Maiha. Wide dirt roads ran beside mud-wall compounds. The huts were roofed with a mixture of grass and corrugated aluminium. We passed the customs post after an amiable

186

chat to the officer in charge.

We proceeded up a rough mountain pass towards the Cameroon border town of Bel-el. However, the road was so bad that when we reached the highest point in the pass we decided to have our picnic there and then return, as by this time, we had travelled about 30 miles along the bush road. We had our picnic under a large mahogany tree, in the upper branches of which were one or two large mistletoe growths in flower. These flowers attracted the attention of a pair sunbirds. The view across the plain was wonderful and the distant mountains from this angle had a moonscape look about them. There was a particularly massive monolith on the plain.

At about 4 p.m. we saw a very high vapour trail and then a high, fast moving, wispy cloud formation piled in from the west and the blazing sun became diffused, is this this the precursor of Harmattan?

Returned painfully along the same route we had come and met some of Heather & Adrian's students en route.

P.M. Anne and Ian, later followed by Jim and Heather, called to say their good-byes to the elderly parents.

### Sunday 6th January

A light harmattan had descended.

7.15 a.m. Adrian and I called for John Button, transferred to John's Land-Rover and bumped off down the Bahuli road for bird watching trip. Ran out of petrol between 4/5 miles.

Decided to walk back detouring along the Mayo Digal river. Many new sightings, including small grey woodpecker with its scarlet cap. What surprised me about this bird was the way it hopped, both feet together, up the vertical tree trunk, the weight of the bird being supported by its tail feathers. At this point observed 59 different species in about 3 hours. We followed a harrier up the river for several miles but were unable to get a positive identification. We also saw our first tawny eagle. By the time we reached civilization, we were all very jaded. We syphoned petrol from Adrian's car and soon had the Land-Rover back.

## Monday 7<sup>th</sup> January

First day of real harmattan, visibility down to 300 yards. It cannot be described as a fog or mist, as it is, in fact, a very fine suspended dust. It drops the temperature mid-day to that of a nice warm English summer's day. The diffused light is however, very eye straining. It makes breathing a little sneezy. We are told that what we are experiencing today is a very bad harmattan and we hope that it does not cancel the Maiduguri/Kano aircraft on Wednesday.

Went to Mubi hospital for Heather to have an injection. Afterwards visited Barclays bank. It was guarded by two police constables armed with old Ross rifles. Heather and Adrian have been informed that teaching will now not start until Wednesday as the boys are arriving back late due to the Salah holiday. Some of the students have come as far as 500 miles and this can take many days.

Many people wandered in to say goodbye. Afternoon went to Kitty and Dick's again. Had hot chocolate with marshmallow and home-made pineapple cake then picked up 14 days' egg supply.

Went to John Button's for a farewell drink. Met a couple of young Nigerian army officers - Jimmy the 2 I/C and his adjutant who had just returned from Aldershot. Jimmy, who lived in the Rivers area of Nigeria, stated that as he was non-Hausa speaking and he was unable to give a direct word of command to his troops as they were non-English speaking. A very pleasant young officer with a somewhat direct approach to problems.

## Tuesday 8<sup>th</sup> January

Very thick harmattan again - farewell to Mubi. Heather has been given official leave to drive us to Maiduguri with

Helen and Ahmadu. Road very bad in places and at one point, only Heather's skilful driving kept us on the road. The Harmattan prevented us from seeing the wild mountain scenery during the first half of the journey. We stopped at the village of Pulka where it was market day. It was here that we were able glimpse the rapidly disappearing traditional Africa. The market was essentially a working market selling food, water, skin bags for carrying water, dried fish etc. To this market came the isolated hill people, the Kanuri and the Shuwa Arabs. Not even simple trading words in Hausa were understood here. Poor Ahmadu did not like the market. We thought he was a little afraid as he walked very close to us all the time. He said on returning to the car "the people are very black here."

A few miles past Pulka the wind veered west and the harmattan lifted, by which time we were on the edge of the wide Maiduguri plain. There is one point several miles long known as The Causeway where the water table is high and the area always floods in the rainy season. Due to this, the road is built up a few feet and this is the only area in Nigeria where winter guinea corn can be seen growing. At each side of the road is a series of Kanuri migrant villages, the temporary nature of the huts being evident from the fact that the normal mud hut walling was replaced by Zana matting. The Kanuri women appear to have two styles of plaited hair, down over the nose if unmarried, and swept up if married.

We next drove through Bama which is well laid out with wide dirt roads flanked by neem trees. The compounds are surrounded by mud walls patterned with a delicate tracery, obviously scored into the mud during the final wall building stage. The Emir's palace was built around the 1930's of local brick. Prisoners supplied the labour at the brickworks and they were much in evidence in their rough white smocks as we passed through.

As the road continued towards Maiduguri a distinct change from arable to stock farming, became apparent.

189

There were a great number of quite large trees. Maiduguri is a peculiar town without any particular form, with a race course (bare and parched) in the middle. There is a massive expansion of educational facilities. The country in the immediate area looks near dessert.

Dropped Helen off at her friends and proceeded to where Heather was staying the night with Jane and Paul, two teacher friends of hers. Here we met a young expatriate, Ian Colurn, and his wife. He works for the Ministry of Natural Resources (Wild Life Division). We discussed what we had seen in Mubi market with regard to Dieldrin. He felt that, whilst the situation was disturbing, the dangers were not parallel with the European/North American situation. Firstly the high temperature coupled with low humidity would tend to break the chemical down and secondly there is no chain of milk products to admit the chemical into the human food chain.

We stayed at the Lake Chad hotel and invited Heather and Helen to dinner; I alone tried the Nigerian dish called Dafaduka Doya which was chicken first boiled then fried in palm oil, it was served with yam and seasoned with very hot peppers.

## Wednesday 8<sup>th</sup> January

This was a disastrous day. There was only a very light harmattan that by 10 a.m. gave way to a clear blue cloudless sky. We were at the airport at 10.15 a.m. for the 11 a.m. flight - all weighed in and waiting. At 1.30 p.m. we were told "No 'plane". Had gigantic row at airport. Went back to Lake Chad hotel and arranged cancellation of that night's booking at the Central Hotel Kano.

Spent the night with Lyall and Marge Watts. Lyall is Deputy Principal of Maiduguri Technical College. In the evening the Principal called in. Mr. Fwa, a most cultured Nigerian and according to Lyall, a very able administrator, was telling us that the authorities are beginning to dilute free education by imposing fees, examination fees and withdrawing or cutting back on travel grants, which Mr. Fwa fears will ultimately lead to an educated elite.

## Thursday 10th January

Most unhappy, clearly more harmattan about than yesterday. Had early breakfast, Heather called for us at 8 a.m. Collected Helen and then on to airport by 9 a.m. Confirmed no plane but Nigeria Airways had been on to North Eastern coach due to leave 9.30. Great rush back to Maiduguri. Coach station like a lorry park. Weighed baggage and paid up with a smile. Heather bought us 4 bananas and a handful of sweets from a passing trader's head. Coach departed on its 330 mile trek sharp on 9.30.

Roads in places terrible, due to extensive re-construction. Several lorries had recently overturned and were lying by the wayside. Harmattan thickening. The first hour was through near desert but improved later with many particularly fine baobab trees of great age and fantastic shapes. Several new species of birds especially starlings could be seen but not positively identified. There were, however, a lot of pintailed whydahs in the early stages of the journey whereas in the Mubi area this bird was not common.

We only stopped three times for 10 min. each. Potiskum about 1 p.m, Kari about 2.45 p.m. and Kachako by which time we were past caring. We did not fancy the fare offered by the roadside - cold fried chicken legs or kebab - both included fly encrustations at no extra cost. Microscopic hard boiled eggs, cola nuts and water out of small narrow-necked pottery water gourds. We declined all these delicacies and stuck to fizzy lemonade to wash down our bananas.

The engine was very ropey and in addition to the three passenger stops we stopped four times for mechanical reasons. On the last occasion the driver and conductor armed themselves with three enormous screwdrivers and a heavy hammer and, after some very robust adjustments,

191

the fault was permanently abated. It could, with those tools, have only been the will of Allah that got us to Kano. About one hour from our destination, I developed the great grandaddy of all headaches.

Arrived Kano around 6.50 p.m. Terrible time with baggage touts at bus station. Thought we were going to lose luggage and get beaten up. Got to hotel 7 p.m. only to find that they had let our reservation go. Great fuss - eventually settled in. Had dinner, retired 9 p.m. exhausted.

## Friday 11th January

Disastrous start. Our flight due 11 a.m. decided not to land due to harmattan. All passengers had been picked up from hotel at 5 a.m. flown onto Lagos, stayed on plane and were due to overfly Kano at 11 a.m. - at 35,000 ft. Next available British Caledonian flight Wednesday. British Caledonian transferred us to Sabina via Madrid and Brussels. Due 12 noon - Kano airport knee deep in pilgrims to/from Mecca. Weighing in, immigration, customs, utter chaos. Plane arrived late accompanied by great cheers from the waiting Baturi. Took off 1.20 p.m. having earlier telexed B.A.C. new flight arrival time.

Wonderful flight north-westwards over desert. Overflew Agades, across the Tamgak mountains, over Tamanrasset, over Mount Tahat area (approx. 10.000 ft.) ending by traversing the high snow-capped Atlas mountains, leaving Africa in the Tangier area. The landscape all the way was quite incredible. Stark, beautiful, sinister and hell-like all at once. Two particular features stand out on the desert leg of the journey. One was a shimmering area of quicksilver, many miles long, as if a gigantic blob of solder had been dropped on the sand from a great height and instantly solidified on impact. The second was a large rock plateau shaped like a piece of a jigsaw puzzle. It was about ten miles across and stood out black amidst the surrounding pink sand.

The views in Spain whilst flying due north over the

barren Sierra Moreno towards Madrid were a breath-taking mixture of setting sun, pink cloudscape, with snow-capped mountain peaks thrusting through here and there. Good landing at Madrid for re-fuelling. Arrived Brussels 7.15. Transferred to Sabina for Brussels/London flight. Ken and Odel met us at the airport, then to their house for a wonderful meal. Nigel and Sandra took us home to Weybridge.

THE GREAT ADVENTURE WAS OVER

# Pregnancy and Childbirth among the Gude
published in The Midwives Chronicle 1979

March 1979 Midwives Chronicle& Nursing Notes

## PREGNANCY AND CHILDBIRTH AMONG THE GUDE

An article by **HEATHER ROSSER**, based on studies undertaken whilst in Nigeria.

Mrs Rosser is now in Botswana, where she hopes to carry out similar research

THE GUDE are a small tribe living in the north east of Nigeria on the Cameroon border. The area is mountainous and until recently the people have had little contact with the outside world apart from other hill-tribes and the Fulanis, who are the dominant tribe in the area. Many of the Gude were converted to Islam by the Fulani and - during the past 50 years many have also been converted to Christianity. However, a large proportion of the older generation are pagan and the traditional beliefs and customs exist side by side with the new. There are several clans within the tribe; my int erest was mainly in the people of one clan who are descendants of the Shuwa Arabs but settled in Lamorde about 200 years ago, after following the hunter Dawa in search of new hunting grounds. His son Kanar established a settlement on Lamorde mountain. Later, his brother moved on to establish another settlement at Gella and his children established the line at Girimburum. It is in these areas that the traditional customs are practised, the people embracing the newer ideas living at the bottom of the mountains, although in villages such as Njari and Sahuda on the main road there is a mixture of beliefs and practices. My interest was in the customs and beliefs related to pregnancy and childbirth, and between May 1975 and June 1976, I took a sample from the villages mentioned above to include pagans, Muslims and Christians, men and women, farmers and "white collar" workers. I was also able to speak to the traditional chiefs of Lamorde, Gella and Girimburum, to a man and woman witchdoctor and to an imam who was a respected leader using Muslim medicine. Finally, I spent some time at the hospital in Mubi talking to the midwives and the ex-patriot obstetrician. I was assisted by Gude students from the Teachers College and Government Comprehensive School, Mubi, who gave up much time not only in accompanying me on my interviews but also in helping me interpret the data afterwards. With the exception of the Gude living in the town of Mubi in small walled compounds, all the people I spoke to were living in large compounds containing several huts and a variety of trees and plants. Each village has several communal wells but all washing is done in the rivers, and people living on the mountain sides usually collect their drinking water from the rivers as it is nearer. The staple diet is guinea corn ground into a mush and served with a soup made from a choice of yakwa and other leaves, okra, peppers, onions, pounded groundnuts, fish and occasionally meat. Fruit trees are plentiful, especially by the rivers. Farming is the main occupation of the people. The work is shared by the men and women; hand hoes are still the most common method of ploughing but ploughs 76 drawn by oxen are also used, and tractors can be hired from the government office in Mubi. Even the people who have other jobs such as pastor, clerk or trader also have some farmland. At planting and harvest time the members of the extended family help each other. In any case a son will often remain in his father's compound when he is married and has children of his own. The average number of children in a family of the people I talked to was five, although often more had been born. Many of the Muslims and pagans had two wives and one wealthy Muslim had four.

**Early Marriage**

Whatever the religion of her parents it is still the custom of girls to marry at about 14 or 15 years unless they are one of the few to attend secondary school. There is more freedom of choice than before, though marriage is still a family rather than an individual affair. After the prospective bridegroom's father has approached the bride's father and the marriage is considered suitable, negotiations to settle the bride-price begin. The dowry, or part of it, is paid a week before the marriage. The actual form of the marriage varies according to the religion of the families but there is always feasting. The bride is then taken to her husband's family compound or to a new compound built near to her in-laws. It is expected that the bride will bear a child within the first year of marriage. A young bride who becomes pregnant rarely informs her husband but may tell a close sister-in-law or friend who then passes on the news. A married woman with several children is more likely to tell her husband if she becomes pregnant but many women said that they keep it to themselves. Once it is obvious that a woman is pregnant she is given special consideration. By the seventh month the woman should stop carrying heavy loads and should not do any heavy farming. There is a variety of opinion as to whether a pregnant woman should eat special foods but several people said that she should not eat sweet things as this would cause a difficult birth. A variety of taboos were mentioned, though the practice of them seems to be dying out and not all were widely known. Many people said that a pregnant woman shouldn't walk at night but only some said that this was because the spirits abroad at night might cause the mother or baby to die. Climbing trees is also taboo, partly due to evil spirits, but also, presumably, for fear of falling- climbing mahogany trees is common amongst pagan women who collect nuts and extract the oil to rub on their bodies. Another taboo is bathing in running water. If the pregnant woman is pagan she may offer prayers to the gods either in her compound or at one of the sacred grottoes or caves on the outskirts of the village. She will also tie round her waist a charm—made for her by a witchdoctor—of powdered medicine twined into a rope of twisted thread and dove feathers. Vomiting during pregnancy is common and the usual cure is drinking tamarind water. The witchdoctor will prescribe a medicine that he makes from herbs and the imam will give the women koranic medicine to drink, a charm and special prayers to say. Several women said that they had received treatment for vomiting at Mubi hospital. The majority of respondents who lived near enough said that they went to the antenatal clinic at the hospital. However, people in Sahuda, 15 miles away, rarely went, and those from Girimburum, accessible only by a three-mile climb up a donkey track from Sahuda, never went. Recently, dispensaries have been established near Sahuda and at Gella but there is no midwife attached. The antenatal clinic does not provide information about labour and the woman pregnant for the first time is not given any advice on how to sit and breathe until she is actually in labour. However, as the majority of women will have witnessed the birth of a baby the experience is not wholly new.

**Place of Delivery**

The actual delivery is the area where there is most uniformity of practice. The majority of babies are born at home but the younger women in particular said that they would prefer to deliver at the hospital if possible. If the woman is expecting her first child she returns to her parents' home to deliver and may remain for any time up to a year after the birth. The most usual place for a mother to be delivered is in her own room but several women said that it depends where the child wants to be born and some babies preferred to be born outside or near the latrine. One woman said that her last baby was born in the kitchen because it was a cold night and there was a fire there. A variety of people may be with the woman during delivery, even her daughter if she is aged over 14, but the person most relied upon is the "old woman". She is often the wife of a blacksmith[1] and may have no formal medical knowledge but she inspires confidence by holding the mother during labour and by attending to the baby immediately it is born. Few people mentioned medicine for pain during labour but if women are in labour for a long time (i.e. over two days) the witchdoctor may be called and he ties a charm around the woman's neck so that she will deliver quickly. It is not the custom for a woman to cry out with pain although she may do so if she wishes. When the baby is about to be born the mother kneels with her buttocks resting against a low stool. A woman standing behind her puts her arms around her waist for support (if the woman has to deliver her baby without help she will try to get to a tree for support) and another woman stands in front of her to catch the child as it falls on to the mat. The baby is not pulled out and some horror was shown when I asked this question. As soon as the baby is born a little water is sprinkled on it to make it cry. Sometimes the baby is given to the mother immediately but in other cases not until the cord has been cut with a razor blade or sharpened corn stalk. Powder mixed with ground herbs and charcoal is then applied to the navel and a bandage is tied around the cord. The "old woman" who attended the delivery puts the afterbirth in a calabash or broken pot and buries it in the compound at the place where the mother takes her bath. Even women delivering in the hospital often bring the afterbirth home to be buried in the compound. Mother and baby are then bathed in hot water, and it is traditional practice to rub both with oil. The baby is wrapped in a new towel and put with the mother on her bed or sleeping mat, except in the case of a first baby when it is given to an older person. The mother is given honey and porridge to eat and later has a meal of specially slaughtered hen or cow's leg. The baby itself will not usually be fed until the mother's milk is ready the following day but it may be given boiled water by hand or, more recently, in a bottle. If the mother does not have enough milk she is given herbal medicine with porridge and the baby is given goat's milk or tiger-nuts ground into a milk-like substance. Nowadays, powdered milk may also be given but it is expensive and obtainable only in Mubi.

**Difficult Births**

Although traditional methods of delivery are successful where the birth is normal people are increasingly relying on the hospital to help with difficult births. One of the problems here is that the relatives will often wait until the mother has had a prolonged labour before taking her on the difficult journey to the hospital. Native medicines may also have been applied before the woman is taken to the hospital. For example there are special herbs that can be soaked in water and drunk if a woman does not expel the afterbirth. Native medicine may also be taken if the mother haemorrhages but there is no medicine known for babies that are born the wrong way, as in a breech or transverse lie birth. The matter is then in the hands of the gods. injections can be given in the hospital to expel the placenta and to stop the haemorrhaging, and caesarean section can be performed if the baby is not in the correct position for a normal birth. If a woman has a normal delivery in hospital she will remain for only 48 hours but she will receive special treatment when she gets home. In the case of a first child the mother will be cared for, usually by her mother, for two months. For subsequent children the mother will rest for seven days but, if her child or children are not old enough to help her, a young relative of her husband's is often called to help. During the two months or seven days the mother is given a special diet to enable her to regain her strength and it is traditional for well-wishers to bring her a chicken. She will also bath twice a day in hot water instead of the normal cold. The father of the child will also help in bringing firewood and water, traditionally the

199

woman's job. There was a variety of opinion as to when the father actually sees the new-born baby. Traditionally he is not present during the birth but two women I spoke to had had their babies so quickly that there was not time to call any help and their husbands had delivered the babies themselves. Although the majority of people said that the husband does not see the baby until the naming ceremony seven days after the birth; several husbands said that they saw the baby as soon as they reached the compound having had news of the birth.

**Important Ceremony**

The naming ceremony is very important, because it marks the point when the child really becomes a member of the family; afterwards the mother is expected to go back to her normal duties, although she will not start farming again until the child is big enough to be carried on her back—at about three or four weeks. The type of ceremony varies with the religion of the family but they are similar in form. Relatives and neighbours are invited to the compound and after the child has been brought from the house by its mother and been formally given its name by an older man who acts as master of ceremonies kola nuts are distributed. Everyone takes kola to show that they wish the baby well. The type of food that is served varies according to the wealth of the family, but it is a custom to slaughter a goat or a ram for the feast. Pagans will also serve burukutu (beer brewed from guinea corn) and there will be traditional singing and dancing. Prayers will have been offered to the gods when the child was named. Muslim naming ceremonies are held in the morning and are quite short affairs. If the child is a boy the imam shaves his head and marks his stomach, if it is a girl her hair is plaited. Prayer for the child is led by the imam, who whispers the name to the child and then announces it aloud. Christian naming ceremonies are longer and held in the evening. There is usually a hymn, a prayer and a reading from the

Hausa Bible before the baby is held by the pastor and officially named. Naming ceremonies are less important than marriages, burials, planting and harvest festivals in Gude culture. But if twins are born the naming ceremony takes on a greater significance. Twins are considered superior people, who have special protection from the gods. Parents of twins are wary about disciplining them in case the gods are angry and seek their revenge by bringing ill- health or misfortune to anyone who does not treat the twins with respect. Although Muslims and Christians no longer fear the birth of twins, pagans still perform the traditional rites when they are born. As soon as they are born twins are placed on a *zana*[2] mat and a slaughtered hen is offered to them so that they will not harm their parents. There is drumming throughout the village to announce the birth of twins and dancing by the men. Even if twins are born to Muslim or Christian parents the pagans in the village will beat drums and shout the news until the naming ceremony. As soon as the twins are born the blacksmith is commissioned to make four small pots, one for each of the twins and two decorated pots which the father keeps, sometimes in a special thatched hut. When the father wishes to appease the god of the twins he offers a sacrifice to the pots. The naming ceremony is much more spectacular than for one child because two of everything have to be provided. Two goats are slaughtered and guests have to bring two presents for the twins; if they don't then misfortune may befall the guest. Feasting and dancing continue long into the night. Mubi is now reached by metalled road and modern ideas from the rest of the country are reaching the town. The hospital, and particularly the maternity wing, is expanding rapidly. Teams of medical auxiliaries now go out into the villages to provide immunisation and health education. With the introduction of universal primary education in Nigeria, primary schools are being established even in the remote areas and health education forms a part of the curriculum. Few educated people retain their pagan beliefs but many of the customs are an integral part of the Gude culture. In their attitudes to pregnancy and childbirth the Gude show that they can incorporate new ideas whilst retaining many of the old traditions.

*1 Blacksmiths are a separate artisan "caste" who practise the specialist skills of ironworking, carpentry, pottery making and medicine. They are regarded with a mixture of respect and suspicion and traditionally intermarry*

*2 Zana mats Woven grass mats up to 2mx2m*

## Bibliography

Barnes, Dr H. F, *"The Birth of a Ngoni Child,"* Man, August 1949.

Erikson, Erik H., *Childhood and Society*, Penguin Books, 1965.

Faw, Chalmer E. (Editor), Lardin Gabas-*A land, a people, a church*, The Brethren Press, 1973.

Freedman, L. Z. and Ferguson, V. M., *"The Question of Painless Childbirth in Primitive Cultures"*, American J. Orthopsychiat, 20, 363—72.

Gideon, Helen, *"A Baby is Born in the Punjab"*, American Anthropology, 64, 1220-34.

lghodaro, Dr Irene, *Baby's: First Year*, Collins, 1966.

Maclean, Una, *Magical Medicine-:a Nigerian case study*, Penguin Press, 1971.

Mbiti, John, *African Religion*, Heinemann. 1975.

Mbiti, John, *African Religion and Philosophy*, Heinemann, 1969.

Meake, C. K., Tribal Studies of Northern Nigeria, Routledge, Kegan,

Paul. 'T' Parrinder, E. G., *African Traditional Religion*, Sheldon Press, 1975

Radcliffe Brown, A. R. and Daryll, Forde (Editors), *African Systems of Kinship and Marriage*, Oxford University Press, I950.

Uka, Ngwobia, *Growing up in Nigerian Culture*, Ibadan University Press, 1966.

# In Time for the Wake
by Heather Rosser

Published in The Bodleian Murders & other Oxford
Stories
OxPens Publishing 2010

The tall Nigerian peered intently at the Benin bronzes in
their glass display cabinet at the Pitt Rivers museum.

"They're amazing aren't they?' said Lisa.

Sam studied the little figures of the king and his retinue
a moment longer. Then he turned and smiled at the young
woman in her jeans and Fair Trade T-shirt.

'My father works in bronze.'

'How wonderful! Does he make things like this?'

He shook his head. 'We live in a village in the Mandara
Mountains. He will sometimes make a mask for a special
occasion but more often it is bells or bracelets or drinking
vessels.'

Sam's words conjured up a picture in Lisa's mind of an
old man sitting in the doorway of a thatched hut, carefully
polishing a bronze chalice. They lingered by a display of
musical instruments and Sam told her about the tradition in
his village of dancing to the drums late into the night
whenever there was a full moon.

Lisa blinked when they came out of the museum into
the autumn sunshine. The leaves on the trees in University
Parks were beginning to turn and by the time they reached
Jericho there was a chill in the air.

'We're nearly there,' she said as she noticed Sam put
his thumbs through his rucksack for support.

'It is very kind of you and your mother to invite me for
the week-end.'

'She's always enjoyed hosting British Council students.
Ever since I was a child the house was full of international
students. That's why I wanted to travel.'

'Have you been to Africa?'

Lisa looked wistful. 'I was hoping to go when I'd paid

204

off my student debt. I worked in London for a few of years and was in the process of applying for overseas posts when my mother had her accident. So I came back to Oxford.' She hesitated. 'You know she's in a wheelchair?'

'No they didn't tell me. I hope I won't be too much trouble.' Sam looked concerned.

'You're the first student she's had since for five years; she's really looking forward to your visit.'

"And I am looking forward to meeting her.' Sam paused. 'What are those people doing?' he asked as they passed a funeral cortege on the other side of the road with half a dozen mourners standing on the pavement.

'It's a funeral,' said Lisa and shivered as a sudden wind chased a flurry of dead leaves along the street. She started to hurry on but Sam stood and watched as the coffin was placed in the hearse and the mourners shuffled into their cars.

'Why are there so few people?' he asked incredulously.

Lisa swallowed. 'Maybe the others are waiting at the crematorium.'

'Where my father lives mourners come from all around to give comfort to the bereaved and help the departed soul on its way. We dig the grave ourselves and they are buried within twenty-four hours.'

'But how do you have time to make all the arrangements?'

'The whole family and neighbours stop whatever they are doing and help. But of course not everyone can be notified, especially in these modern days when many people are away from home. That is why a wake is held a year later.'

'A wake?'

'Yes, that is the time when all the family come together and a final feast is held for the departed. Sometimes,' Sam explained earnestly, 'a soul has difficulty in getting to the other side but when a wake is held the departed knows that their time on this earth has ended.'

'It sounds a good way to honour the dead,' Lisa said

thoughtfully.

***

Frost scrunched beneath her tyres as Lisa cycled past the Sheldonian and came to a halt at the Oxfam shop. She locked her bike and paused to admire the colourful Christmas window display before opening the shop. A woman hurried in for wrapping paper, a calendar and some Fair Trade chocolate. It was early but Lisa didn't have the heart to turn her away and she knew the volunteers would be arriving soon. Managing a charity shop hadn't been in her mind when she graduated with a business degree but the opportunity had arisen soon after she returned to Oxford to look after her mother and she found the work both challenging and satisfying.

She glanced appraisingly at the displays of jewellery and exotic gifts, then went upstairs past neat rails of clothes, before hurrying up the final flight and into a room piled high with boxes of donated clothing, books and bric-a-brac waiting to be sorted. She crossed the room and opened the door to her office. While she was waiting for her computer to boot up she looked out of the window. Students were hurrying to lectures and a traffic warden was already patrolling cars parked on the Broad.

She turned back to her computer and was soon absorbed in sales figures while the volunteers got on with serving customers and checking stock.

'The post has arrived.'

'Thank you, Mary.' Lisa smiled as she took a bundle of envelopes from a small grey-haired woman.

'How's your mother today?'

'She seemed a bit better this morning,' Lisa paused, 'But the doctor who came yesterday said it was still touch and go.'

Mary nodded sympathetically as Lisa flicked through the envelopes.

'There's one with a Nigerian stamp. Oh, it's from

Sam.'

'The student who stayed with you?' Mary's voice had a soft Oxfordshire burr.

'Yes.' Lisa scanned the letter. 'Oh dear!' she said as Mary was leaving the room.

'Not bad news?'

'His father died of a heart attack.' Lisa frowned. 'And Sam didn't get back in time.'

'I'm sorry for your friend.' Mary touched Lisa lightly on the shoulder as she left.

\*\*\*

Lisa glanced across at Trinity College but was unmoved by the colourful hanging baskets and the multi-lingual exclamations of delight from tourists.

Since her mother's death on New Year's Day, she had felt suspended in time.

She had the support of friends and colleagues but she came from a small family and her relatives were all distant. Throughout the summer she felt weighed down by loss. Previously she had enjoyed watching graduates throwing their caps in the air when they spilled onto the Broad fresh from receiving their degrees. But the hugs from proud parents were too painful and she kept the window firmly shut.

\*\*\*

The autumn air was chilly as Lisa cycled home through St Giles.

'Watch where you're going!'

She rang her bell and swerved to avoid a fresh-faced student wobbling on his bike as he gazed up at the historic buildings. She pedalled furiously, angry with herself for shouting but resenting the optimism of the undergraduates teeming into Oxford for the start of Michaelmas term.

Her heart was palpitating by the time she reached the

little terraced house she had shared with her mother and was now hers. As she was locking her bike she noticed a parcel tucked behind the recycling box and her mood lightened when she saw the Nigerian stamps.

She took the package into the kitchen and opened it carefully. Inside was a bronze mask about the size of her palm. The eyes were hollowed and the lips had been fashioned so that they looked soft despite the hardness of the metal. The nose was broad and the nostrils flared. The full cheeks had cicitrations similar to those Lisa had noticed on Sam's face.

Still holding the bronze, Lisa tore open the envelope and read Sam's letter. He said he was back in his village making preparations for the wake. The mask was the last thing his father had made before he died and he wanted Lisa to have it as a memento of the weekend he had spent in Oxford and as his tribute to her mother.

Tears ran down her cheeks as she placed the mask on the table but she brushed them aside and determinedly chopped vegetables for a stir fry. As she cooked, her eyes were drawn to the mask and she picked it up, cradling it in her palm. She kept it by her plate as she ate, occasionally tracing the outline of the features with her finger.

Lisa took the mask into the sitting room and wondered whether to light the fire. Instead she slumped onto the settee and switched on the television, flicking channels till she found a travel programme about Africa and, soothed by the sonorous commentary, drifted off to sleep.

She woke to the sound of canned laughter and felt a spasm of pain around her heart. She shuddered and stood up, the mask now heavy in her hand. Her mouth felt dry and she walked towards the kitchen breathing rapidly. Another spasm gripped her and, clutching her chest she turned, dropping the mask into the fireplace. It lay in the grate almost hidden in the cold ashes. Lisa touched her forehead and was surprised to find she was drenched in sweat. She glanced at the telephone, wondering if she should call anyone but decided she was simply over-tired and would have an early night.

She dreamt of an unfamiliar face half hidden behind a waterfall dappled by sunlight and felt a great tiredness as strange voices whispered in the shadows.

It was dawn when she sat bolt upright, suddenly wide awake. She hurried downstairs to the sitting room and started scrabbling in the fireplace. Her heart began to pound when she saw the bronze face in the ashes. She picked it up, raising a cloud of dust. Hesitantly, she studied the mask but its features were blurred with ash. She blew away the dust from around the eyes then started on the nose giving short quick breaths. As specks rose from the nostrils she almost felt as if she were giving the kiss of life. When she looked up at the mantelpiece she saw the smiling photo of her mother and carefully put the mask on the table.

Lisa turned on the radio and switched on the lights. By the time she was ready to leave for work she had thoroughly cleaned the kitchen and felt able to face the day. She wheeled her bike down the garden path then stopped, certain she had forgotten something. She went back into the house and looked around the living room. The mask lay on the table and, scarcely aware what she was doing, she stuffed it in her bag.

\*\*\*

'Hello, Lisa. How are you today?' Mary put her head round the office door.

Lisa opened her mouth to say she was fine then pressed her hand on her chest as she was seized by another spasm.

'Are you all right?' Mary's face was full of concern.

'I'm fine, just a touch of indigestion.'

'I'll get a glass of water.'

When Mary returned Lisa was holding the mask.

'What a beautiful piece.' Mary put down the glass. 'Where did it come from?'

'Sam sent it to me. His father made it.' She stroked the

209

cheeks then gasped and grimaced in pain.

'Lisa, you're not well.' Mary handed her the glass.

Still holding the mask, Lisa sipped the water.

'How long has this been going on?'

For a moment Lisa said nothing. She looked across to Trinity College garden, resplendent in shades of autumn, and remembered Sam's visit nearly a year ago.

'It only started yesterday.' She frowned. 'After I opened the parcel.'

Mary looked serious. 'May I look at the mask?'

Lisa hesitated then reluctantly handed her the bronze.

Mary sat down. 'Thank you.' Her expression was unfathomable as she studied it then her eyes closed.

Lisa felt confused and wondered if she had fallen asleep.

'I can hear running water,' Mary said. 'There is a compound surrounded by a high cactus hedge. In the compound are several huts. There is an old man sitting outside the largest hut, he is making something ***'

Her voice trailed off and she winced sharply. She shook herself, screwed up her face in concentration and continued.

'The old man is sick. I can see a shadow over his head. I get the impression the man is working against time, there is something he wants to finish before he goes.'

The room was quiet as Mary sat silently for few minutes longer. Then she opened her eyes and looked into Lisa's wondering face.

'Sam told me his family have a cactus hedge round their compound.'

'And I remember you saying that his father died?'

'Yes, almost a year ago, of a heart attack. Sam said the mask was the last thing he made.'

'A heart attack, yes I can feel it. And now this poor troubled soul is imprisoned in his craft and struggling to get back to his native land.'

'I don't understand.' Lisa stared at the ordinary looking woman in front of her who seemed to be having some sort of vision.

Her mind wandered back to a conversation she had had with Sam, 'Sometimes a soul has difficulty getting to the other side but when a wake is held***'

'The wake!' Lisa held out her hand for the mask. 'Perhaps it needs to be back for the wake.'

Mary nodded. 'I think it's sending you a message.'

'What should I do?'

'Maybe you should send it back.'

'I'll think about it.'

***

'Do you think I'm doing the right thing?' Lisa asked as she and Mary joined the queue at the post office.

'I'm sure you are.'

'Cashier number five please!'

Lisa shuffled to the counter. 'This parcel is very heavy,' she said, cradling it in both hands.

'Pass it through please'.

Lisa reluctantly handed the parcel to the cashier.

She gave Lisa a strange look as she put it on the scales. 'It's less than a kilo.'

'Is that all? I'd like to send it express.'

'That will be considerably more than ordinary post.'

'It's important.' Lisa's fingers trembled as she punched in her card details. She watched the cashier drop the precious parcel in the mail sack. Then she felt Mary's arm around her as they walked away.

'It's on its way now,' she said quietly as they went out into St Aldate's.

***

Lisa was very tired for the next few days but the chest pains had gone and she felt less angry when she saw people enjoying themselves.

211

A week after she posted the mask, she heard the sound of drums outside the shop. She looked out of the window but there were just the usual parked cars, bicycles and a tourist bus.

She looked again and felt herself gathered up among a throng of brightly clad people singing and dancing to the beat of drums. Her office was filled with tropical heat and fragrant smells.

The door opened and she turned startled eyes towards the intruder.

'What's the matter? You look as if you've seen a ghost,' said Mary.

'I think I have,' Lisa said simply.

She looked out of the window again. The scene returned to normal but the sun had come out and for an instant she saw her mother's face.

And for the first time in months she felt at peace and ready to embrace her future.

# The Bronze Chalice

Sitting cross-legged on his grass mat the Blacksmith
Chips away the clay mould with infinite care.
Squatting beside him, his Grandson watches
Mesmerised, as glimpses of bronze are revealed.

Oblivious to the sun's heat, swishing of tall grasses
And murmuring of women's voices as they pass
Balancing pots on their heads,
The Old Man painstakingly continues his work.

All afternoon the Boy watches, creeping closer,
Spellbound as an exquisite bronze chalice is revealed.
Cupping it in his hands the Grandfather
Solemnly gives it, his final creation, to the Boy.

His eyes widen as he gazes at the
Intricate carvings around the rim and the
Tiny pillar on which the chalice stands.
'I will keep this forever,' he whispers.

The Old Man shakes his head.
'Cherish it well till the time is right
To let the spirits within it pass to another place
As I will soon pass on to join our ancestors.

Many moons later in the City of Oxford
A story-teller delves into his Box of Things
And holds up the chalice
For eager children to imagine its story.


*Heather Rosser*

Published in Poems in an Exhibition
an anthology of poems inspired by art in support of
Standing Voice
Oxford Folio 2017

*The chalice was a gift when I left Mubi, NE Nigeria in 1976 after four years. It was made using the lost wax process which involves moulding an object in beeswax and covering it in clay, leaving a small hole. The beeswax is removed by heat and the cavity filled with brass. Recently I passed on the chalice to my son-in-law who is a children's author.*

Lightning Source UK Ltd.
Milton Keynes UK
UKHW01f0223110618
324036UK00002B/47/P